Why I Am a United Methodist

Why I Am a United Methodist

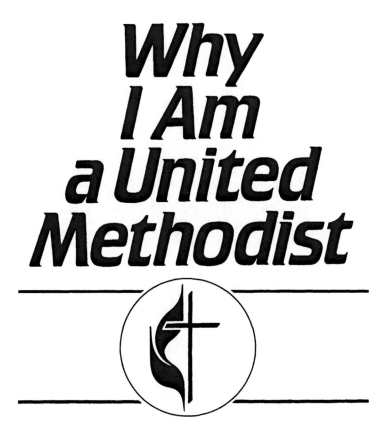

WILLIAM H. WILLIMON

ABINGDON PRESS

Nashville

WHY I AM A UNITED METHODIST

This book is printed on recycled, acid-free paper.

Library of Congress Cataloging-in-Publication Data

WILLIMON, WILLIAM H.
Why I am a United Methodist / William H. Willimon.
p. cm.

ISBN-13: 978-0-68745-356-6 (alk. paper)

1. United Methodist Church (U.S.)—Apologetic works.
2. Methodist Church—Apologetic works. I. Title.
BX8331.2.W53   1990
287'.6—dc20   89-27339

Scripture quotations in this publication unless otherwise noted are from the Revised Standard Version of the Bible, copyright 1946, 1952, 1971, 1973 by the Division of Christian Education of the National Council of the Churches of Christ in the U.S.A., and are used by permission.

All Scripture quotations marked KJV are from the King James Version of the Bible.

"When in Our Music God Is Glorified" (quoted on p. 61) copyright © 1972 by Hope Publishing Co., Carol Stream, IL 60188. All rights reserved. Used by permission.

11   12   —   22   21

MANUFACTURED IN THE UNITED STATES OF AMERICA

In memory of the Reverend Bessie B. Parker,
Servant of the Servants of God
in
the South Carolina Conference of
The United Methodist Church

Contents

INTRODUCTION

If you ever travel between Greenville and Mauldin in upcountry South Carolina, take the little side road that lies midway between them and crosses just below the Reedy River Dam, the winding road that leads to the rather forlorn mill village called Conestee. Almost at the top of the hill that overlooks the river and the village is a one-room, eight-sided brick church. The sign out front will tell you that this is "McBee Chapel United Methodist Church."

In the early 1800s "Shouting Methodists," as critics then called us, built a number of these curious octagonal churches around the country. Now, only a handful remain. Elders at McBee Chapel explained the odd little building by claiming that the church was built in an octagon because "somebody found out that an eight-sided corn crib held more corn, so an eight-sided church could hold more people." We Wesleyans have been nothing if not practical.

Soon after someone built a mill on the river at Conestee, Methodists arrived and built a church. Anywhere across the continent of North America where there were people, they were immediately followed (and sometimes preceded) by the loud-singing, Bible-preaching, hard-riding Circuit Riders. The little octagonal church at the top of the hill in Conestee is the legacy of one such traveling preacher.

My family had been members of McBee Chapel since its founding. There, on the back of a pine pew, my brother carved "Roy Rogers" during a particularly long sermon. Family legend disputes whether it was due to my mother's dozing or paying so close attention to the sermon that she did not see what my brother was doing with his pocket knife. There, on a summer Sunday, I was baptized and thereby made a Christian called Methodist. Most of our United Methodist churches resemble McBee Chapel, not in architecture but in spirit. Sixty percent of our churches have fewer than two hundred members, and there are more of them than United States Post Offices in out of the way places like Conestee. In fact, although the Post Office has given up and left Conestee, the United Methodists haven't.

While I was still too young to know I was a Methodist, my family moved its membership to the large, downtown Buncombe Street Methodist Church in nearby Greenville. There, in that vast, neoclassical, downtown cathedral, the work begun in me at McBee Chapel was brought to completion so that I came to answer quite naturally to the name, Methodist, and have ever since.

Because you have no intention of ever visiting Conestee, South Carolina, you wonder why I tell you this story of my ecclesial origins. I do so to admit, right here at the beginning, that my honest response to why I am a United Methodist is admission that I am a United Methodist today because ordinary Christian people at McBee Chapel and Buncombe Street made me one.

It may sound strange for me to admit that I didn't choose to be a United Methodist. Would my spiritual journey seem more interesting if I could tell you that I became a United Methodist only after a long, tortured process of reflection, investigation, and study? If I examined all possible denominational options and found the United Methodists to be the most credible and Christian? Although I have known people who could claim that, I can't. I am here because I was put here.

My involuntary placement among the United Methodists doesn't bother me a bit. We Americans often exalt freedom of choice. We like to think of ourselves as independently derived, self-made men and women who are who we are because we decided and chose to be that way. Religion isn't really yours unless you found it all by yourself, on your own, choosing it as individually right for you.

Our glorification of our power of choice overlooks the fact that so many of the really important things in our lives—our looks, our name, our family, our tradition—have come to us not through our choosing but rather through the choices of others. So many of the really important things about us have come to us as gifts. Another word for gift is "grace." We are who we are by grace rather than through our individualistic achievement or choice.

So if I believe, if I still answer to "Christian" when called, it is mainly because someone else told me the story, lived the gospel before me in places like McBee Chapel and Buncombe Street Church in ways that made me know that this was my story, my name, my salvation.

James B. Duke, who founded Duke University, where I now preach, explained his philanthropy by saying, "My old daddy always said that if he amounted to anything, it would be because of the Methodist Circuit Riders. If I amount to anything, it will be because of the Methodist Church." Since I have been at Mr. Duke's University, in daily contact with both chaplains and students from a variety of denominational and religious backgrounds, I have come to see how much of a United Methodist I really am. Sometimes we United Methodists like to believe that we are pretty much like everyone else. Being a lone United Methodist in the middle of everyone else has given me a new appreciation for our United Methodist distinctiveness. We really are different. I have enjoyed writing this book because it has given me an opportunity publicly to testify (we Methodists have always been big on testimonials) to the debt that I owe to this church. Why am I a United Methodist? I am that way because of a gift, because of grace.

The church which flowed from John Wesley's experience at Aldersgate Street in London and spread like wildfire across a continent through places like McBee Chapel, has now covered the globe with its message of God's grace to ordinary people. This book is not so much a collection of United Methodist doctrines or an outline of our history, although I shall try to identify those aspects of our history and beliefs which are most interesting. This book is one person's account of the ways in which that United Methodist version of Christianity has made and continues to make a difference to me and to so many others. Today United Methodism has over 9 million members, 38 thousand congregations and 37,500 clergy in our 73 Annual Conferences. On a given Sunday, over three and a half million of us make it to church. All this is an act of God's grace and, as we United Methodists love to sing, God's grace is nothing less than amazing.

Grace means gifts, and gifts imply indebtedness. Here is my acknowledgment of my own indebtedness to people whose names I can't even remember in places like McBee Chapel and Buncombe Street Church, to all those believers who followed John and Charles Wesley in their revival of the Church of England and continued that revival here in the churches of the Evangelical United Brethren and the Methodists which eventually became The United Methodist Church we love today.

> William H. Willimon
> Duke University Chapel
> Pentecost 1989

CHAPTER ONE

BECAUSE RELIGION IS OF THE HEART

The United Methodist Church is the lengthened shadow of an eighteenth-century priest in the Church of England—John Wesley. To know us well, you must first meet Mr. Wesley and his hymn writing brother, Charles. The brothers Wesley grew up in, what would be to our minds, a curious home. Their father, Samuel, was a church of England clergyman in Epworth. Like a number of clergy I have known, Samuel Wesley was always in financial trouble. Although he fancied himself as somewhat of a poet, he had a rather undistinguished career. It is odd that we latter-day Wesleyans have always been big on keeping extensive and accurate records for our church because, Samuel Wesley's family record keeping left a bit to be desired. His records do indicate that his son John was born on June 17, 1703, but no one can tell for sure whether he was the thirteenth or the fourteenth Wesley child. (Who's counting after nine or ten?)

John Wesley's mother, Susanna, was much more exacting than her husband in her guidance of her children. Susanna was one of the strongest influences on John's life. A person of independent mind and spirit, she had strong opinions on most subjects, though her health suffered from the bearing of 19 children. In Methodism, Susanna Wesley is regarded as the mother of the movement (although contemporary United Methodists are a bit embarrassed by Susanna's boast that she taught her children to fear the rod and to cry softly!). Susanna once gave mothers advice concerning childhood diet: Children should be given as much weak beer as they wanted but must never ask for anything at the table. "I insist upon conquering the will of children," she said. The Lord's Prayer was taught each Wesley child as soon as the child could speak, and all of her children (except for poor, sickly sister Kezzy) at age five were taught the alphabet (in one day), and the basics of reading (in one day).

Life in the Epworth rectory was no island of tranquility for the Wesleys. Samuel tended to stir up trouble in the parish. One night in 1709, the rectory caught fire and the family barely escaped. The last to be rescued was little John. Later biographers looked back on John's close encounter with death as a sign of divine providence. He was "a brand plucked from the burning" (cf. Amos 4:11, Zech. 3:2) for special work. The terrible fire was of suspicious origin. So at an early age the Wesley boys learned that religion can stir dangerous passions and that church people are not above meanness.

After the fire, while the rectory was being rebuilt, the Wesley children were farmed out to the homes of sympathetic parishioners. When the family was finally reunited, Susanna complained that they had been allowed to play "with any children, good or bad . . . to neglect a strict observance of the Sabbath, and got a knowledge of several songs and bad things, which before they had no notion of," including "a clownish accent and many rude ways" which "were not reformed without some difficulty."

In her high regard for the families of her husband's parish, Susanna reminds me of my father-in-law, a United Methodist pastor, who, when asked, "Preacher, why are ministers' kids always so mean?" replied, "Because they must play with the children in the congregation."

While the boys, Samuel, Charles, and John, received the best education that England had to offer, as was the custom of the day,the seven surviving Wesley sisters, Emilia, Susanna, Mary, Mehetabel, Anne, Martha, and Kezia, received only rudimentary instruction and domestic training. They were confined to poor marriages and drab lives, taking little interest in the religious movement their brothers led.

John Wesley was not a simple, uncomplicated person,and no one ever claimed that he was an easy person to live with. Domestic tranquility was not high on his personal agenda. Could that be why he devised a church structure which made the church itself into a new family?

Let's be honest. Great people are sometimes so busy changing the world that they fail to take care of business at home. During a painful sojourn to Georgia in 1735–37 (painful both for the young Mr. Wesley and the colonists to whom he was sent to serve), Wesley courted Miss Sophy Hopkey. While nothing shocking occurred between them, Wesley revealed then his enduring ineptitude in domestic matters. (It was said that, for recreation, when he really wanted to show her a good time, Wesley read Miss Hopkey edifying works on church history.) When she dropped him for another man and Wesley retaliated by barring her from taking Holy Communion (by invoking a fine point of church discipline against her), the rough Georgia colonists turned against the rigid, high-church, fastidious Mr. Wesley. A disheartened Wesley headed back to England moaning, "I went to Georgia to convert the Indians, but who shall convert me?"

John Wesley had an unfortunate marriage that is not discussed much among us. (Two weeks before his wedding, he addressed his preachers on the desirability of clerical celibacy. Should he have followed his own advice?) "I did not leave her, I did not send her away, I shall not call her back," was John Wesley's sparse comment upon the departure of his unhappy wife.

None of this family gossip can account for the mid-course change that was to take place in Wesley's life. As a student at Oxford, Wesley displayed an early and unusually intense desire to deepen his spiritual life. He was greatly influenced by a book on spiritual discipline, William Law's *Serious Call to a Devout and Holy Life.* Law invited people to become serious about their religion, to develop certain habits and practices which would keep the mind more continually focused upon God. Such discipline was most attractive to the young Mr. Wesley, who was troubled in spirit and searching for some means of reassurance of the state of his own soul.

John Wesley had a reputation for being a methodical person as far back as these student days at Oxford. If Methodists are methodical we got the madness of our method from Wesley. He began an extensive program of self-examination, spiritual pulse-taking, and self-reform, devising long lists of temptations including "reading vain plays," "light behavior," and, above all "idleness".

In 1732, Wesley gathered five or six Oxford friends who shared his commitment to highly disciplined Christian living and formed the Holy Club. A storm of criticism was heaped upon Wesley a few months later when one of the young men died, allegedly as a result of the fasting and extreme ascetic practices of the Holy Club. "Methodism" was a term of contempt by which bemused observers described the odd, systematic spiritual exercises and methods of his Holy Club.

In turmoil after his father's death, Wesley went to Georgia to minister to the colonists and Native Americans there. It was a futile expedition in which the punctilious Wesley only alienated the very folk he was supposed to be serving. On the way back from his frustrating missionary sojourn in Georgia, in 1738, the unhappy Mr. Wesley came in contact with Moravians, a German pietistic sect which stressed the need for an inner, personal assurance of salvation. Their firm, assured faith reminded Wesley of how uncertain was his own faith. "What must I do to be saved?" The question of the rich young ruler (Luke 18:18) was the question that tormented Wesley. He was still working on the assumption that an assurance of salvation, knowing he was a true Christian, was mostly a matter of affirming correct beliefs and performing appropriate actions.

While still off the coast of England on his way home from Georgia, Wesley confided to his *Journal:*

> It is now two years and almost four months since I left my native country in order to teach the Georgian Indians the nature of Christianity. But what have I learned myself in the meantime? . . . that I who went to America to convert others, was never myself converted to God. . . . I "am fallen short of the glory of God"; that my whole heart is "altogether corrupt and abominable." . . . That "alienated" as I am "from the life of God," I am "a child of wrath," an heir of hell. . . . I have no hope. . . . The faith I want is, "a sure trust and confidence in God, that, through the merits of Christ, my sins are forgiven, and I am reconciled to the favor of God. . . ." I want that faith which none can have without knowing that he hath it. . . . (*The Journal of the Rev. John Wesley, A.M.,* Nehemiah Curnock, ed., [London: The Epworth Press, 1938] Feb., 1738)

His personal assurance of salvation was to come a few months later in London in May of 1738 (just three days after his brother Charles reported "a strange palpitation of the heart" on Pentecost which enlivened his faith). John now felt that he met the criteria for being a "true

Christian" which had been set by his Moravian friends. Here is his account of his life-changing, heartwarming experience at Aldersgate Street:

> In the evening I went very unwillingly to a society in Aldersgate Street, where one was reading Luther's preface to the Epistle to the Romans. About a quarter before nine, while he was describing the change which God works in the heart through faith in Christ, I felt my heart strangely warmed. I felt I did trust in Christ, Christ alone for salvation: And an assurance was given me, that he had taken away *my* sins, even *mine,* and saved *me* from the law of sin and death. (*Journal,* May 24, 1738)

Now Wesley made his own the Moravian idea that until one has experienced personal, heartfelt assurance of salvation, one is only "almost Christian." Although Wesley still had seasons of spiritual depression (just seven months after Aldersgate, Wesley honestly revealed to his *Journal* that "I am not a Christian." No spiritual "high" inoculated a self-searching person like Wesley from periods of doubt), something really changed for Wesley in his heartwarming experience. For Wesley, and consequently for United Methodists, Aldersgate Street is not just an address in London; it is a watershed mark in the history of the Christian faith. Although Wesley never forsook the great doctrines and creeds of the church, vigorously defending every point of Anglican doctrine against any attack by those who would water down the creeds or the Anglican Articles of Faith; although Wesley never retreated from and in fact deeply intensified his commitment to good works as the outward expression of inner faith; after his Aldersgate experience, Wesley wedded to doctrine and service an *inner, heartfelt experience of the saving grace of God.*

As an Anglican, Wesley already knew and used three

means of determining Christian belief: scripture, tradition, and reason. Because of the influence of his own faith journey at Aldersgate, and of the Moravians, Wesley added a fourth test—*experience*. Later this religion of the warmed heart touched a German Reformed pastor named Philip William Otterbein, who in mid-eighteenth-century America came to a similar consciousness of salvation. With Martin Boehm, Otterbein founded the Church of the United Brethren, one of the churches comprised in United Methodism.

Today, United Methodism demonstrates its pietistic roots when we stress the need for every person to experience the love of God in a way that is personal, convincing, and transforming. Before Aldersgate, Wesley knew in his head that Christ had died for him, forgiven him, and loved him. After Aldersgate, Wesley knew Christ *in his heart*. The externals of religion—going to church, putting money in the offering plate, working in the church's soup kitchen for the poor, standing and affirming the Apostles' Creed in worship, reading the Bible—are all essential. But for us as heirs of Wesley and Aldersgate, internal appropriation of faith—heartfelt, personal assurance of God's love in *my* life, *my* heart—is the first essential.

It is necessary to have my name on a church roll somewhere. It is important that I know and understand as much of the Bible as possible. It is valuable for me to show forth my faith through acts of love and compassion. But somewhere, someday in my life I must be able to say yes—yes to God in the deepest, most engaging way, yes in response to my experience of God's yes to me in Christ.

This isn't a United Methodist requirement. It is a United Methodist *gift*. People, even people who are not Christian, know that religion is nothing if it is not some force which enlivens me at the deepest core of my being, if it is not faith which is more than just truth in general for most people but which is truth experienced particularly by *me*, in me.

So people sometimes say things like, "It doesn't really matter what you believe as long as you are sincere"—a really misguided statement when you think about it since it *does* matter whether what you believe is true. Surely they don't mean that it's a virtue to believe a lie. What they mean by appealing for sincerity is that religion ought to bring truth down off cloud nine, down to earth, down to me and my life, grip me firmly, turn me inside out, work me over. It ought to be *experienced*.

That's what the Christian faith became for Wesley that night at Aldersgate Street. The fastidious little, Oxford don who knew all *about* Jesus, came *to know Jesus*, experienced truth personally, as a person, a person who "had taken away *my* sins, even *mine*, and saved *me* from the law of sin and death."

In the third chapter of John, a man named Nicodemus comes to Jesus by night and asks what he needs *to do* to get in on what Jesus is selling. Jesus replies, "Unless one is born anew, he cannot see the kingdom of God" (John 3:3). Old, successful, high-achievement Nicodemus is understandably befuddled. After all, he has always earned and achieved everything he ever wanted in life. What must he *do* to get this new birth? How is it possible for an old man like me to be born a second time? he wants to know. Can I enter the womb of my mother and try to get born one more time?

Jesus replies, "The wind [*pneuma*, spirit] blows where it wills."

See? Nicodemus, like the young Wesley, thinks that religion is primarily something he does, something he must work hard to believe, or some good deed he must try hard to perform. But the kind of birth Jesus describes is not something we believe or do, it's an act of God, a gift of

God, *grace.* So Jesus refers to wind (the same Greek word for spirit). You don't create or control the wind. Nor do you control God's Spirit. It "blows where it wills." Here is something, this new birth, you can only have as a gift. Grace.

Actually, the Greek word used by Jesus in talking with Nicodemus about birth doesn't really mean "anew" or "again." The word *anothen* means literally "top to bottom." "Old codger, you must be born from top to bottom," Jesus tells Nicodemus.

Naturally, Nicodemus wants to know how in the world Jesus proposes to teach an old dog like him such new spiritual tricks. "The wind blows where it wills," promises Jesus. The spirit can touch any life, even yours.

That night at Aldersgate, in a dull church meeting that John Wesley attended only with great reluctance, he got reborn from top to bottom. From that night on, Wesley never stopped preaching about the need, no the *gift,* of the "new birth." At our best, we United Methodists have never stopped preaching it either. We must—*no, we can!*—be born again. No one is too sinful, too old and set in his or her ways, too wise, too confused, or too dead to get a new birth. And it all comes as a gift. Grace.

GRACE FOR ALL, GRACE IN ALL

We Americans are achievers; hard-working, success-minded, goal-oriented people. There is no free lunch, we say. You get what you pay for. To our ears, the notion that our salvation, our relationship to God is pure gift, sounds strange.

So Jesus told stories of a prodigal son who wasted his inheritance in loose living in the far country, yet was given a party when he returned home; the eleventh-hour worker who was paid the same as these who labored in the vineyard all day; the great banquet where the invitation went to those who had never been invited anywhere in their whole lives.

After a lifetime of relentless self-examination, continuous effort, extreme rigorousness, and other attempts to get close to God, John Wesley came to the stunning realization that God had already come close to him, was waiting for him, to embrace him, eager for the party to begin. Grace.

It was this amazing grace of God which his brother Charles expressed so exuberantly in a beloved Methodist hymn:

> Depth of mercy! Can there be
> mercy still reserved for me?
> Can my God his wrath forbear,
> me, the chief of sinners, spare?
>
> I my Master have denied,
> I afresh have crucified,
> oft profaned his hallowed name,
> put him to an open shame.
>
> There for me the Savior stands,
> shows his wounds and spreads his hands.
> God is love! I know, I feel,
> Jesus weeps and loves me still.

Thomas Langford writes that "the grace of God, as the redeeming activity of divine love, is the center of Wesley's theology. The themes Wesley emphasized came from his conviction that God's gracious love is the dominant reality in human life. Definitively expressed in Jesus Christ, grace covers the entirety of life: It creates, redeems, sustains, sanctifies, and glorifies" (Thomas Langford, *Practical Divinity: Theology in the Wesleyan Tradition*, p. 24). Wesleyanism can be thought of as a concrete, institutional, and personal embodiment of the power of God's love. Throughout his thousands of sermons, Wesley is primarily concerned with encouraging people to respond to God's gift of grace in Jesus Christ by making a personal choice for the way of God in Christ over the ways of the world, and then to live out that choice in their daily lives. He had contempt for those who were "almost Christian," the person who was a "natural man." This new birth is more than some decision we make, more than a New Year's resolution or turning over a new leaf. It is a sign of the work of God through Christ in our lives. It is free in all and free for all. It does not depend upon any merit or striving on our part, good emotions, or good desires. Whatever good that is within us is a gracious work of God.

Both Charles and John felt that experience of the grace of God was at the center of Christian existence. No one preached grace better than John; no one sang about grace better than Charles in his immortal hymn "Jesus, Lover of My Soul":

> Plenteous grace with thee is found,
> grace to cover all my sin;
> let the healing streams abound;
> make and keep me pure within.
> Thou of life the fountain art,
> freely let me take of thee;
> spring thou up within my heart;
> rise to all eternity.

Admittedly, our Wesleyan emphasis on love and grace can be perverted into a kind of mushy, all-affirming inclusiveness, open to everything and rejecting nothing. This is certainly not true of Wesley and is not true of us United Methodists at our best. In a success-oriented, achievement-infatuated society, this stress upon grace sounds strange to many ears. Yet we, like Wesley, see the experience of God's grace at the very center of the Christian faith.

One of John Wesley's most descriptive phrases was "grace for all, grace in all." The first part of the phrase means that Wesley believed that no one can be excluded from the operation of God's powerful grace—no one, be that person a prodigal son, a stuffy Oxford prig, or a dusty Bristol miner. No one. This argued against the Calvinist idea of limited election: some but not all are saved. The second part reveals his conviction that grace is right now at work in every human being—right now, even as you read this. Wesley described this working of grace in three primary ways.

Warning. The rest of chapter 1 deals with Wesley's main theological contributions. Although the material which follows may not be as interesting as hearing about John Wesley's days with Sophy Hopkey, it is much more worthwhile. So please don't be put off by the use of strange words like "prevenient" and "sanctification." You need to know these words if you are going to be an informed United Methodist. Besides, it will be fun to use them around your Presbyterian and Lutheran friends who think that United Methodists don't know any theology.

Prevenient Grace. This is one of the most distinctive United Methodist doctrines. We believe that from the beginning of a life, God is busy working in that person's life. The image of God is never completely erased in an individual, no matter how bad that individual is. Prevenient grace may precede any direct consciousness of God, any great awareness that one is being led by God, coaxed toward salvation.

No one, whether that person knows it or not, is immune from the proddings, enticements, and flirtations of God. Once again, Wesley's own experience served as a basis for his assertion of prevenient grace. Looking back upon his life up to Aldersgate—the rescue from the parsonage as a child, the rather too glum rigors of the Holy Club at Oxford, the frustrating sojourn as missionary in Georgia, even those nagging friends who wouldn't take no for an answer the night of the meeting at Aldersgate—Wesley could now feel an unseen hand, a deep, loving, guiding presence. Prevenient (literally "coming before") grace.

Charles Wesley remembered the story of Jacob's wrestling with the angel (Genesis 32) and interpreted it as a story about the way that the unknown God comes to us, preveniently steals in upon our lives, wrestles with us, and ultimately wins us by love:

> Come, O thou traveler unknown,
> whom still I hold, but cannot see
> My company before is gone,
> and I am left alone with thee;
> With thee all night I mean to stay,
> And wrestle till the break of day.
>
> I need not tell thee who I am,
> my misery and sin declare;
> thyself hast called me by my name,
> look on thy hands, and read it there.
> But who, I ask thee, who art thou?
> Tell me thy name and tell me now.
>
> Yield to me now, for I am weak,
> but confident in self-despair!
> Speak to my heart, in blessing speak,
> be conquered by my instant prayer.
> Speak, or thou never hence shalt move,
> and tell me if thy name is Love.

'Tis love! 'tis love! Thou diedst for me,
I hear thy whisper in my heart.
The morning breaks, the shadows flee,
pure, Universal Love thou art.
To me, to all, thy mercies move;
thy nature and thy name is Love.

Justifying Grace is that first awakening, that "new birth" to one's salvation, the initial, life-changing experience that sets us on the road back to God. Jesus says that, in the far country, the prodigal son "came to himself"; he remembered his waiting father and home (Luke 15). The father was his father all along. But now, in this moment of joyful recognition, the son *knew* him as *his* father. At Aldersgate, Wesley experienced God's justifying grace. Jesus had justified humanity to God nearly two thousand years before. But that night Wesley *knew* that Christ "had taken away *my* sins, even *mine.*" So a chief Wesleyan emphasis is *assurance of salvation.* Probably because of his own misery before Aldersgate, Wesley believed that people ought not to cast about, perplexed and confused about their fate with God. The church, our fellow Christians, the Bible, and all the other means of grace exist to bring us to a firm, conscious, resolute assurance that God is there for us and loves us with an unwavering, eternal love. At Aldersgate, justifying grace worked in Wesley to give him "an assurance," that he was saved, loved, forgiven, elected, and cherished by the love of God.

And well might the story of grace have ended with Wesley. After all, isn't the point of Christ's incarnation, and his death on the cross, to reconcile us to God, to set things right between us and our Creator? Unfortunately, in much American evangelical Christianity, this is where the grace appears to end. Too many evangelicals tirelessly reiterate the first steps to salvation, the initial awakening, justification with little attention to what happens next. Where do we go the morning after an Aldersgate experience?

Sanctifying Grace is the continuing presence of God's work in our lives after our conversion. The grace, the gifts don't stop. God has surprises in store for us still. We may now be fully Christian, that is, fully accepted, forgiven, reconciled. But God isn't finished with us yet, not by a long shot. God may take us, as we United Methodists love to sing, "Just as I am, without one plea," but God never leaves us just as God found us.

Often some United Methodists speak of Wesley's Aldersgate experience as if that were the *end* rather than the *beginning* of Wesley's journey. That account of Wesley ignores the significant moves that continued to occur in his life and thought after Aldersgate. He kept revising his sermons and pamphlets, trying this new procedure and that one. Wesley's most enduring, far reaching contributions to the church occurred long *after* Aldersgate. In other words, God's grace kept working in him.

John Wesley used the terms "Christian perfection," "holiness," and "sanctification" almost interchangeably. Sanctification was sometimes called a "second work of grace" or a "second blessing." Holiness means the state of being holy or sinless. Sanctification refers to a condition of being free from the power of sin and restored to the image of God. Those are bold claims. Is this state possible for Christians?

"Entire Sanctification or Christian Perfection," writes Wesley, "is neither more nor less than pure love; love expelling sin, and governing both the heart and the life of the child of God. . . . Indeed what is more or less than humble, gentle, patient love!

"There is no perfection," he said, "which does not admit of a continual increase. So that how much soever any man has attained, or in how high a degree soever he is perfect, he hath still need to 'grow in grace,' daily to advance in the knowledge and love of God his Savior." ("The Great Privilege of Those That Are Born of God," in *The Works of John Wesley*, Jackson, ed. [Grand Rapids, Mich.: Baker Book House, 1979] pp. 223-33.) Wesley's distinctive contribution, then, was that he considered this doctrine of sanctification as a practical way of life available to and necessary for every dedicated Christian. Christians are to grow. Grow in grace.

In the Bible, the word "sanctification" means to set apart something and make it holy, to commandeer something or someone for special use by God. At Aldersgate, John Wesley, who wanted so desperately to be holy, to be used by God for good, was commandeered by God, sanctified. He continued to examine his habits, life-style, speech, and behavior. He continued to rise early for prayer and Bible reading, to visit regularly at the prisons. But now he did so as one on the way and urged his followers to do the same.

This Wesleyan emphasis on sanctifying grace is perhaps our most distinctive contribution to the picture of Christian life. Yes, it makes United Methodists appear awfully concerned about personal behavior, ethics, life-style issues, social justice, and much busyness in doing good. But our stress upon sanctification is the way we embody—personally and institutionally—our faith. This is the concrete, everyday way we link our love for God to our commitment to justice for our neighbors.

In his small groups, the societies, bands, and conferences (which we will discuss later) Wesley's followers examined one another and encouraged one another to "grow in grace." Our historic stress upon Christian education is an outgrowth of our living out of sanctifying grace. We believe that even ordinary people—like you and me—can grow, can end up better people than we would have been if left to our own devices, can "go on to perfection."

Perfection? Yes. An outgrowth of Wesley's experience of continuing, sanctifying grace was his stress on "Christian perfection." He took seriously Jesus' invitation to "be ye therefore perfect as your Father which is in heaven is perfect" (Matt. 5:48 KJV). By "perfection" Wesley did not mean moral flawlessness or utter sinlessness. He meant perfection in the sense of maturity. By God's grace (and only by God's grace) we can (even utterly ordinary folks like us) make progress. We can end up looking better, more complete, more mature and perfected than when we began. With God's help, we really are offered the promise that we are getting somewhere, so far as our lives with God are concerned.

The notion of Christian perfection means more than the smug and simple, "We are getting better and better, every day, in every way." It may mean that we mature in our assessment of ourselves, that we grow in our awareness of how sinful and inadequate we really are! After Aldersgate, Wesley became more, not less, astute and careful in his assessment of his own life.

Nearly thirty-five years after Aldersgate, Wesley wrote to Charles, "I often cry out, *vitae me redde prior!* [Let me return to my former life!] Let me be again an Oxford Methodist! I am often in doubt whether or not it would not be best for me to resume all my Oxford rules, great and small" (*Wesley's Letters*, Frank Baker, ed. [Nashville: Abingdon, 1984], Dec. 15, 1772) "Going on to perfection" did not mean that Wesley knew no walk through the valley.

Going on to perfection means that, through God's sanctifying grace, we grow in our idea of God, letting go of childish and unsound images of God. Our faith becomes more complex, better able to withstand the buffeting of life. We grow in our commitment to serve

God. We take on new challenges in Christian service which require greater spiritual maturity and energy of us. As Paul says, "When I was a child, I thought, I spoke, I acted like a child. When I became an adult, I put away childish ways" (I Cor. 13, author's paraphrase).

Christian perfection is at the heart of the strong ethical emphasis of United Methodism. Wesley defined Christian perfection as a gift from God which made a difference in our everyday behavior. Christian perfection is "to offer up every thought, word and work as a spiritual sacrifice, acceptable to God through Christ. In every thought of our hearts, in every word of our tongues, in every work of our hands, to show forth His praise who hath called us out of darkness into His marvelous light. O, that both we, and all who seek the Lord Jesus in sincerity, may thus be made perfect in one" (John Wesley, *Christian Perfection*, Thomas Kipner, ed. [New York: World Publishing Co., 1985], p. 36).

Sometimes, in the debate on the floor of one of our Annual Conferences, a motion is made on some issue. Then the whole Conference gets into the act, offering suggestions, criticisms, amendments to the motion, all with the intent of "perfecting the motion." Nobody believes that when all the dust of debate settles our motion will be flawless, the best piece of legislation ever written in the history of democracy. What we believe is that, due to the gifts offered by the whole body in "perfecting the motion," we will have a much better, a much wiser motion than when we began.

We United Methodists believe that, through grace, God is busy working the same sort of perfection in us, even us.

The experience of God's grace in its prevenient, justifying and sanctifying forms is a hallmark of United Methodism, an aspect of our (in Wesley's phrase) "experimental [meaning *experienced*] Christianity."

What we have experienced in our hearts issues forth in the work of our hands, shows forth for all to see like salt and light.

Beginning at Aldersgate, continuing through the Bristol coal fields, even to places like McBee Chapel, this "religion of the warmed heart" has, by the grace of God, ignited every corner of a cold world with its unquenchable fire.

A couple of years ago, I was teaching in a school of theology of the German church in Bonn, West Germany. We were discussing theology (as German Christians love to do). Most of the students were speaking about the need for a reasonable, clear, well thought out faith. I agreed, but added that emotion, feeling is also an important dimension of religious experience. Now, the Germans are deeply suspicious of emotion. Their experience during the *Hitlerzeit*, the "Hitler Time," has convinced many of them that emotion can be dangerous, demonic. I see their point. My point was that emotion, like any human gift, can be used for good or bad. The feeling evoked by the experience of God's grace in Christ is quite different from the nationalistic fervor evoked by Adolph Hitler. Feelings must be tested by the Bible, trained and evoked through confrontation with the Gospel, I said. My German friends were still suspicious.

Finally, my German host professor broke into the discussion. *"Er ist ein Methodist,"* he explained to the students. He is a Methodist. Yes. That explains it. I'm a United Methodist. I really do believe that religion is, whatever else it is, a matter of a heart strangely warmed, a life impassioned as an offering to God.

CHAPTER TWO

BECAUSE THE BIBLE IS OUR BOOK

"The thing that I like about being a United Methodist," said the man on the third row from the front, "is that you can believe pretty much whatever seems right to you personally."

"Well look," she said, "I'm a Baptist, you're a Methodist, but the main thing is not so much what you believe as long as you are sincere, right?"

As you now know from reading chapter 1, these opinions about "the people called Methodist"—although held by lots of people—just happen to be wrong. Believing whatever seems right to you personally has little to do with believing as a Christian, and a belief is not right simply because somebody sincerely believes it. Adolph Hitler was as "sincere" as John Wesley, except that one man lived and died by what was true whereas the other lived and died by a lie. While clear thinking isn't the answer to every problem in life, it is possible for people to be in misery, not because their hearts are not right or because they are bad people but because they are confused. If people become confused at a cloverleaf intersection, think how much more confused they are apt to be about God.

Our church invites us, as United Methodist Christians, to think about God. Thinking about God is called *theology* and all of us do it even if we don't know that's what we are doing because everybody tries to make sense out of life, wonders what we are doing here, and would like to know where we will be tomorrow. So there are no nontheologians; there is just good theology and bad theology.

But where do we begin? On what basis do we make theological judgments? Here's what our *Discipline* says: *"United Methodists share with other Christians the conviction that Scripture is the primary source and criterion for Christian doctrine. Through Scripture the living Christ meets us. . . "* (p. 81).

Read Nehemiah 8:1-10. A strange, long forgotten scroll has been found in the walls at Jerusalem during a renovation. It is a Torah scroll, a collection of "the law of Moses which the LORD had given to Israel." Ezra assembled the whole nation at the Water Gate (stop snickering, please), and at the Water Gate, Ezra stood in a special pulpit and read aloud the whole law. Most had never heard it. It had been lost during years of turmoil and exile. The people heard again those ancient words, "Hear, O Israel; The LORD our God is one LORD ; and you shall love the LORD your God with all your heart, and with all your soul, and with all your might (Deut. 6:4-5).

The people wept when they heard the law, when they heard again what God wanted of them. They wept tears of repentance and confession. Israel's faith is a religion of speaking and listening. God speaks. They listen. This is God's Chosen People at their best: hearing the law of God, listening, aligning their lives accordingly. You get this biblical religion in Luke 4. Jesus returns to his hometown synagogue in Nazareth and what does he do? What Israel does every Sabbath—he picks up the Torah, God's law; he reads; he interprets.

Torah, law, the gospel represent for biblical people like Israel—like us—the "overagainstness" of God. Judaism and Christianity are not religions we find in our hearts, or discover in nature walks in the woods, or stumble upon by thinking long thoughts in our study. These religions come to us as *a word from the outside*—in an ancient scroll found buried in a wall; in the sermon of a young Nazarean prophet back home from college for the weekend; in a changed Oxford don preaching to rough Bristol coal miners. In such moments we are reminded that our God is a real God, not some projection of our collective imagination. Our God stands over against us, outside us, beyond us. Our God's ways are higher than our ways, God's thoughts are deeper than our thoughts. We have to be told what this God wants of us. Somebody has to speak it to us. Luther called this the *verbum externum*, the "external word." Paul once said, "Faith comes from hearing."

I did not say that this word coming from God through people was always a comforting, pleasing, easy word. When this external, over-against, divine word came upon the people that day at the Water Gate, they wept. They wept at the gap, the great chasm between our ways and God's ways. Sometimes, when Wesley preached, people heard him gladly and were deeply, wonderfully moved. Sometimes, his preaching made them so mad that they wanted to kill him, and came close on a couple of occasions. But pleasing or angering people is not the point behind this biblical word. The point is that we are brought near to God's truth for us, be it pleasing or maddening.

We United Methodists have inherited a beautiful Covenant Service out of the Wesleyan tradition which is sometimes used at the beginning of a New Year. The words of that service state well the demand made upon us by being a people who dare to listen to God's word:

> *Christ has many services to be done; some are easy, others are difficult; some bring honor, others bring reproach; some are suitable to our natural inclinations, and temporal interests, others are contrary to both. In some we may please Christ and please ourselves; in others*

*we cannot please Christ except by denying ourselves. Yet
the power to do all these things is given us in Christ who
strengthens us. (The Book of Worship, p. 387)*

To be a United Methodist Christian is to be one of
those who have come forth from the mass of humanity to
listen to the word of God, as revealed by and contained
within the Bible, and have aligned their lives accordingly.

For Wesley, the Bible is not simply a collection of
burdensome divine commands. The Bible is the joyfully
consistent testimony of God's never ending Grace and
ever seeking love. That is why the two principal
resources that Wesley left for his followers for theological guidance were his *Sermons* and his *Notes on the New
Testament.* When he preached, most of his sermons were
a string of biblical quotations.

Wesley's revival is proof of German martyr Dietrich
Bonhoeffer's assertion in *The Cost of Discipleship* that
every

revival of Church life always brings in its train a richer
understanding of the Scriptures. Behind all the slogans
and catchwords . . . there arises a quest . . . for Jesus
Christ himself. What did Jesus mean to say to us? What is
his will for us today? How can he help us to be good
Christians in the modern world? . . . let us get back to
Scriptures, to the word and call of Jesus Christ himself.
(R. H. Fuller, trans. [New York, The Macmillan Co., 1966]
p. 67)

Now it sounds all well and good that we United
Methodists should be people who read, study, and honor
the Bible. Being for the Bible is much like being for
motherhood and apple pie. Who wouldn't be for the
Bible? Yet, in placing the Bible at the center of our

theology, we are engaging in risky, dangerous, counter-cultural activity.

One year, in early December, I was in my office, talking to one of my parishioners about some problems in her life. She was telling me how much conflict she was feeling over what to do with her life. Should she turn this way or that way? "Preacher," she asked, "what I should I do?"

Fortunately for her, I am a seminary-trained pastor. I've had courses in pastoral counseling. So I responded to her as I had been taught, displaying my great sophistication and good pastoral counseling technique: "Well, what do *you* think you ought to do?"

Isn't this the purpose of counseling? You come to me as your pastor, and I try to help you find out the answer to what ails you in you. I'm not here to preach or scold, I'm not even here to give answers. I'm only here as a kind of therapeutic midwife to help you to find the answers to what ails you in you. Right?

Then it hit me. In just a couple of weeks I was going to stand up in front of a congregation and tell a familiar but still odd story of how, after waiting for thousands of years for us to cure what ails us through our own devices, God finally resorted to his own devices. One night at Bethlehem, God stole into human history and laid an "answer" on our back doorstep. The story of Christ's nativity is *not* an account of how we finally got ourselves together, got organized, and worked out our own salvation. The story is about how what God wanted to do for us was so great, so loving, so completely beyond the bounds of human striving or imagination that God had to come here and do it for us, resorting to virgin birth, angels, and the like, or it would not have gotten done.

At last the Holy Spirit got my attention, grabbed me by the collar, and shook me up and down. ("Are you all right, preacher?" my parishioner asked.) The difference between coming to your preacher for help and going to your local psychiatrist is not just that one charges you an arm and a leg while the other does it for free. The difference is that your preacher offers help in the light of a strange story called the gospel which is witnessed to by this strange book called the Bible.

You may think that the toughest task of a Christian is serving on your Church's Finance Committee without losing your faith. No. Your toughest task as a Christian is to hold your life and your church accountable to this peculiar, odd, not made for television story called the gospel.

The solution to what ails you is *not* found first in you. It is found wrapped in swaddling cloths and lying in a manger. And every day you have to jump out of bed, turn off the alarm, brush your teeth, and remind yourself that you live in the light of this peculiar story and not some other. The world has a stock of competing stories, alternative saviors, rival accounts of how we live and move and have our being. As United Methodist Christians, we live by a story called the gospel. This doesn't mean that the Bible is a rule book. On many issues in life, the Bible will not tell you exactly what to do. But the Bible is helpful in placing us in the right context whereby we can begin to ask and to answer our questions as Christians, as believers who feel that our lives are supported by and held accountable to the purposes of God.

In my town we had a debate over the morality of homosexuality. How ought we to think about sexual ethics? Some fundamentalist Christians quoted the Bible on the subject. "Homosexuality is wrong," they said. Now, although this has been a much discussed topic for us, it is of rather little import for the Bible. You can count the verses which are (possibly) concerned with homosexuality on one hand; to tally the number of verses in the Bible on the dangers of wealth requires a computer.

At any rate, one of our theology professors at my seminary wrote a letter to the newspaper, in response to all the letters by the fundamentalists, to inform the good Christians of Durham that, "the Bible cannot be used to construct a sexual ethic." This came as a shock to many. "The Bible is a culturally conditioned book," the theologian explained, "limited by prescientific thought." In other words, aren't we lucky that we know more than the Bible?

A few days later, a person wrote in to respond to the theologian's letter. "While I don't have a Ph.D.," he said, "and I'm only a layman, while I've never taught at the university, spent all my life as a janitor, I think I'll take the Bible a bit more seriously than the learned theologian. She writes about faith from the safe vantage point of a tenured chair at the university. These Bible people wrote their words in blood."

The Bible is a culturally conditioned book. True. But *we* are culturally conditioned people. It is usually easier to see the Bible's cultural blinders than our own. Any time I stand up and say that sexual morality is a private, personal matter, that the important thing is not what tradition or the community says, but what feels personally right to me, I'm not doing theology. I'm no more than mirroring my own cultural limitations. I didn't say that merely by turning to the Bible you will find an easily identifiable, one-to-one Bible "answer" to modern ethical problems like abortion or homosexuality or nuclear power. But you will find something better even than answers—namely, you will find the context, the vantage point from which Christians move to answer our questions. Thus the Bible has a way of putting us in our place, a specifically Christian place which is prior to our answers.

When I was in seminary we were told, in homiletics

classes, that the tough task of the preacher was "to preach with the Bible in one hand and today's newspaper in the other." Get it? The preacher is the one who must heroically work to bring this old, primitive, prescientific world of the Bible to bear on this brave, new, modern world. The task of theology is to make Christianity credible to the modern world. Our best theological minds have been enlisted in that task of translating the old, outmoded, irrelevant world of the Bible to the wonderful, new, scientific, modern world. How can we make the old Bible credible to the new, modern world?

I remind you that this brave, new, wonderful, modern world gave us not only the telephone and the television but also Auschwitz, Hiroshima, and the extermination of Native Americans. This is the modern world which biblical people are supposed to take seriously?

So our United Methodist theological statement asserts that, "As we open our minds and hearts to the Word of God through the words of human beings inspired by the Holy Spirit, faith is born and nourished, our understanding is deepened, and the possibilities for transforming the world become apparent to us" (*The Book of Discipline*, p. 81).

For too long the traffic has been moving in one direction on the bridge between our modern world and the world of the Bible. As United Methodists, heirs of Wesley, at our best we have not been interested in adapting the Bible to the world. Rather, we took as our mandate nothing less than the adaptation of the world to the Bible. The Bible is not as much a roadsign at an intersection as a *collision*. When reading the Bible, at home in private or on Sunday among brothers and sisters in the church, we come to a head-on collision with our preconceptions and limited, self-centered opinions. As our theological statement puts it, *"The Bible serves both as a source of our faith and as the basic criterion by which the truth and fidelity of any interpretation of faith is measured" (The Book of Discipline, p. 82).*

So John Wesley took great pride in saying that he was "a man of one book," though he certainly read more than the Bible. In saying that the Bible is primary, we are saying, with Wesley, that the task of being a Christian is the tough, daily, increasingly difficult challenge to take the Bible a little more seriously and ourselves a little less so.

Our main problem is not to "clean up" the Bible so that it is worthy of being affirmed by a skeptical modern world. Rather, our chief task is the formation of a faithful people worthy of the Bible. Our *Discipline* asks us to "open our hearts and minds to the Bible." The modern mind likes to think of itself as open-minded. In reality, the modern mind has flattened the universe to a one-dimensional, human-centered reality where what might be is usually defined on the basis of what already is and the primary human task is adjustment to the status quo rather than open-minded imagining of a new heaven and a new earth. When we are at our best, dealing with scripture is mind-blowing.

A young man came in to see me and said that he thought he was losing his faith. I asked him about his major. "Philosophy," he said.

"That explains it," I said. "You've been running around with the wrong crowd. But what is this 'faith' that you are losing?"

"I no longer am able to believe in the virgin birth of Jesus," he said.

"Well, what is it? Tuesday? I seem to believe in the virgin birth today, but who knows where I'll be on Wednesday? The point is not what you or I happen to believe, it's what the church believes, the Bible asserts. Relax, maybe it will come to you when you are older."

"But how can I be a Christian when I can't believe this doctrine?" he persisted.

"Look, I hate to tell you, but the virgin birth is not the strangest thing we are going to ask you to believe."

"Really?"

"Really. No, next we're going to ask you to turn the other cheek rather than turn violent, to look across a communion table and believe these strangers are sisters and brothers, to start thinking that the poor and the outcast are really royalty. We start you out on the virgin birth because we think if you can believe that without choking, we can eventually get you to swallow the really important, really essential stuff about Jesus."

Come to us and we will, as our theological statement says, open up your little heart and mind and slap you with possibilities they don't tell you about on the 6:30 news.

We can only act within a world we can envision. The modern world, with its rather myopic world view, tends to produce people who make small, cautious moves in life because their vision doesn't reach much further than the limits of their own egos. So most of us settle down and keep low. Even little moves scare us.

Jesus preaches a sermon which begins, "Blessed are you poor . . . blessed are you hungry . . . blessed are you persecuted . . . blessed are you unemployed . . . oh how fortunate are those of you going through marital distress . . . " (Matt. 5, author's paraphrase). The congregation does a double-take. Blessed? Fortunate? What is this? In our world, when you are poor, you are treated like a nobody, a failure. When you are unemployed, people avoid you like you have some kind of social disease.

The preacher says, "Oh, excuse me, I should have been more clear. I'm not necessarily talking about the American way. I am talking the kingdom-of-God way. In this new, inbreaking kingdom, the poor shall be royalty, those whom you consider outcasts and failures are at the center."

How shall they hear of this kingdom without a preacher, a biblical preacher?

So, in the same Sermon on the Mount, when the preacher talks about turning the other cheek, not repaying evil with evil, offering the shirt off your back and your coat as well, the preacher talks like this as a means of getting our attention, calling us to see a new kingdom.

Of course, you know how we usually respond to such Bible talk. "Jesus didn't really mean that we should turn the other cheek. That's impossible, unrealistic, just Bible talk." So we quickly dispose of the big Bible vision and embrace more acceptable, attainable visions. We adapt the Bible to suit ourselves rather than adapting ourselves to suit the Bible. This is a peculiarly un-Wesleyan response. The truly Wesleyan biblical question is not, How can we create the Bible to suit our limitations? but rather, How can we create a church which will enable us to overcome our limitations when dealing with the Bible?

John Wesley could have said to himself, "Well, these eighteenth-century English people are poor, not too well educated, biblically illiterate, victims of poverty and addiction. What can anybody do?" But Wesley didn't do that. What he did was to create structures to enable ordinary, everyday people like you and me to be people worthy to hear and embody scripture. John Wesley's societies, class meetings, and conferences, which are discussed in chapter 7, were his creative invention where ordinary, everyday people got to deal with the Bible, not as an intellectual problem but rather as a social, political, personal *challenge to transformation.* Wesley's societies were a political response to the serious call of scripture—making a biblical people out of ordinary folk.

Rather than asking how can we blunt the edge of Scripture to suit our limitations, Wesley asked what sort of church it would take to produce people who are able to be non-violent, nonmaterialistic, courageous and bold.

The most pressing biblical interpretation question in our own day is also a political, social, structural, and ecclesial question: What sort of church would we need to be to make *me* a living, breathing, visible disciple of Jesus?

Bishop Richard B. Wilke, after visiting hundreds of our churches and studying church growth and decline says,

> Authentic vitality seems to pulsate where a congregation is most in harmony with the apostolic witness. The early Christians knew that their lives had been changed. They were able to share their experiences so that others could become followers. The apostles focused on preaching, teaching, healing, and prayer. Churches that use helium balloons or live camels in the Christmas pageant or strobe lights on the pulpit do not hold the key. Authentic biblical Christianity is working. Look for signs of life, and you will generally find honest, straightforward New Testament Christianity. "And with great power the apostles gave their testimony to the resurrection of the Lord Jesus, and great grace was upon them all" (Acts 4:33).

The United Methodist Church was born out of this stunning vision, this creative collision between Wesley's eighteenth-century England and the Bible. Our church stands today at that frightening, potentially invigorating collision, challenges you and me to be biblical people not only in our thinking but also in our living, and invites us again to do some creative thinking about the church in the light of the Bible's vision of whom we ought to be.

George works sixty hour weeks in the heart of one of our nation's great cities. By day, he is on the staff of a church and community sponsored clinic for people with

AIDS. By night, George walks the streets looking for intravenous drug users, talking to them, giving them literature about how to prevent AIDS. On weekends, he is usually speaking on the AIDS epidemic in a church, usually in a United Methodist church. So I asked him, "George, what led you to give your life so totally to this work?"

He looked a bit sheepish, as if his answer to my question was going to sound dumb. "Why? Well, I was in church on Sunday. The preacher read the story about how Jesus called little Zacchaeus down out of the tree, how Jesus went to dinner with him. Of course I knew the story since childhood, doesn't everyone? Well, the preacher noted how Zacchaeus, though he had lots of money, was an outcast, someone who was despised by the community. Yet Jesus reached out to him, linked himself with him, ate with him. The preacher remarked, just as a kind of side comment, 'If you want to be with Jesus, you'll usually find him with the outcasts.' And I thought about AIDS, about the suffering of these people. I thought to myself, 'Where would Jesus be if he were walking the streets of our city?' "

It was, for George, as if a revelatory scroll had been found after having been buried in a wall. The Word of God had become God's word for George personally.

In our United Methodist preaching, in our reading and study of the Bible, when it is at its best, it is a wonderful, devastating encounter with the living God, A collision, something akin to a scroll being discovered after being long hidden in a forgotten wall.

CHAPTER THREE

BECAUSE RELIGION IS PRACTICAL

So the Bible is our primary source for doing theology. But what difference does it make to United Methodists that scripture is primary for us? There are other churches and theological traditions which would agree that Scripture is primary. By that they mean that the Bible is a repository of great religious ideas that one is supposed to get one's head straight about, and that's what makes you a Christian. This way of thinking is revealed in statements such as this: "Here are six fundamentals, derived from scripture, which you must affirm to be a *real* Christian."

United Methodism is *not* that kind of church. When we say the Bible is primary, the criterion by which we judge ourselves, we do so in a way which can only be described as *practical*. We are interested in what the Bible *says*, and we encourage our scholars and teachers to wrestle with that and help the Bible speak to us in our day. But more than what the Bible *says*, we are interested in what the Bible *does* to us in our day through the power of the Holy Spirit. As our Theological Statement puts it: *"Our theological task is essentially practical. It informs the individual's daily decisions and serves the Church's life and work. . . . Our interest is to incorporate the promises and demands of the gospel into our daily lives"* (*The Book of Discipline*, p. 79).

When my colleague Tom Langford wrote his survey on theology in the Wesleyan spirit, it was no accident that he entitled his book *Practical Divinity*. That's how John

Wesley described his own theology—practical divinity, practical theology. When Wesley was a student and his father gave him advice about all the learned theologies he ought to read, his mother added a note that she preferred that Wesley keep his theology "practical." John usually did what Susanna asked. One of the main things that interested Wesley about theology was not only what theology says to people but what it does to people. Theology for us United Methodists is not just talk about God, or a string of certain interesting ideas about God. Theology is our way of creating a people of God.

Sometimes we Americans give the word "practical" a bad name. We are practical, utilitarian, pragmatic people which means that we judge all persons and experiences on the basis of the old American paradigm, "What good will this do me? What practical, real-life consequences will this have for me?" Practicality can be vulgarized into the notion that what works is what's best. Sure, they have a Karate for Jesus Exhibition at their 11:00 A.M. worship service and offer a free pair of panty hose to whoever brings a visitor to Sunday school but it works! And what pragmatic, utilitarian American can argue with what works?

When we United Methodists say that we're practical Christians, we mean that we believe that our faith should be put into practice. Warmed hearts must become active hands. Theology was for Wesley never an end, but rather a means for developing and transforming lives. Theology was to be preached, sung, and lived.

The critical theological issue for Wesley was the tension that exists between (1) salvation by holy living and (2) salvation by faith alone. Here's the problem with which Wesley struggled: If salvation is granted as a free gift of God's grace, apart from what we do, and at times despite what we do, then of what value are good works and the disciplined life that Wesley stressed? Wesley's great theological challenge was to hold these two poles together. Holy living had always been a concern of Wesley's. But after Aldersgate, he knew in his own heart that we are saved by the grace of God and nothing else. However, our faith is embodied in love. Spiritual rebirth is a gift of God which results in a new life that expresses love of God and neighbor.

Wesley realized that the Reformation tendency to polarize "faith alone" and "holy living" was a distortion of the Christian message. He was convinced that the two must be held together. While Wesley turned out "rules" by the dozens for his people, he also warned that even the most scrupulous rule-keeping would only get you to the state of being an "almost Christian." Even though he devised creative means for Christian growth such as highly developed, intensive small group worship and prolonged, therapeutic methods for Christian maturity, he never lost sight that salvation is first a work of God in us. Thus Wesley pulled off a rather amazing theological feat. He managed to repudiate both the righteousness of arrogant works, and human self-assertion and, at the same time, advocate prolonged practical means for achieving Christian maturity. He affirmed God's amazing grace in saving us sinners without encouraging a lapse into ethical passivity.

Wesley's linkage of both grace and good works was an achievement in theology something like the winning of a national championship in basketball is in athletics.

MAKING DISCIPLES

Toward the end of Matthew's Gospel, Jesus gives his disciples their marching orders. He tells them to, "Go therefore and make disciples of all nations, baptizing . . . , teaching. . . . " (Matt. 28:19, 20)

Just in case anybody thought that following Jesus was

something that comes naturally, an inborn inclination, a matter of nice people gradually becoming a bit nicer, Jesus settles all that in this Great Commission. Disciples are not born. You have to *make* disciples.

The way Jesus invites us to walk is a narrow way, so against the stream, so uncommon that anything less than intentional, careful, Christian formation will not do. If being a Christian were merely a matter of breathing the air and drinking the water, absorbing a little godliness by osmosis, then we wouldn't need the church, wouldn't need help from our friends. We could be Christian the same way that people become a Rotarian or a member of the Women's Garden Club. We could hand them a membership card and a lapel pin rather than half drowning them by baptism.

From all that we know of Jesus and his demands upon us, being a disciple of his is a good deal more demanding than the completion of a pledge card and the right hand of fellowship. Discipleship requires a lifetime of commitment, trial and error, struggle, correction, prayer, and a host of virtues which cannot be had simply by wanting them. The great God reaches out, grabs us, accepts us, just as we are, warts and all, long before we get around to reaching out to, and accepting God (Prevenient Grace). God is doing a serious, life-changing, total renovation when he comes after us. When God begins work on us (Justifying Grace), what he has in mind is more than a paint job and a new front porch. God is planning a complete, basement-to-attic overhaul which will cost us an arm and a leg (Sanctifying Grace).

The amount of effort required helps to explain why the word *disciple* is related to the much more troubling and decidedly old-fashioned word *discipline,* a word which evokes bad memories of your third-grade piano teacher, Coach Smith with the whistle around his neck, and boot camp days at Fort Bragg. We're not much into discipline these days, are we?

But it is unimaginable that one could be a disciple, could follow a master whose name is Jesus, without discipline—the conscious, intentional submission of our feelings, time, talents, and projects to the will of God as revealed in Christ. Disciples are made, not born.

Unfortunately, discipline isn't plentiful these days. What abounds is freedom, or at least what we call freedom. What we call freedom is the maximum amount of space to do whatever it is that I jolly well want to do. We have "freedom of choice," which means that I am set loose to choose a maximum number of options for my life. But on what basis shall I choose, and to what end? Ah, there's the rub in our freedom.

My society—the affluent, upwardly mobile, American society, that is—enables me to be free, to decide, to choose, to roam at will. But it gives me absolutely no help in deciding what is worth having, on what basis my freedom of choice becomes interesting, truly freeing, and the free exercise of the best of my humanity. My society tells me that I'm free, but it cannot tell me what to do with my freedom. So, left to my own devices, I merely lunge toward whatever craving I have at the moment. When asked what I'm up to, I'll tell you that I'm "meeting my needs." However, since I have no coherent view of myself beyond the bounds of my momentary desires, no goal in my mind for my life beyond what I feel like I might want right now, what I call "need" is mostly an amorphous bundle of desire, a self-indulgent, ever-changing blob of ego.

Little wonder that increasing numbers of our fellow Americans report that, even in this supposedly most free of all nations, they feel anything but free. They feel trapped, hemmed in by a growing government bureaucracy (when a nation has no goal or vision, it must settle for rules and those who administer them), chemical addiction, irresponsible parents, selfish children, and an endless treadmill of buying, consuming, and craving. I once heard that George Bernard Shaw defined Hell as that place where you *must* do what you now only *want* to do. Having now unlimited freedom to express our sexual, economic, intellectual, and political desires without the constraints of any notion of a higher value, God, or anything beyond the simple fact that we want to, we live in something that feels very much like, well, . . . *Hell.* An over-sexed society is just another manifestation, like an over-consuming economy, or an overly bureaucratized state, of our dilemma of being all decked out with our rights and our freedom with absolutely nowhere worthwhile to go.

Reaction to unlimited freedom suggests that we may be the first generation in a long time to have confidence in old-fashioned Wesleyan *discipline.* To be a disciplined person is to be someone who has some means of being able to say yes and to say no (no small achievement in a self-indulgent age). Without some goal, some vision of the good beyond the confines of the moment or our own egos, we tend to say yes to everything out of fear that we might say no to the very thing that would make our lives worth living. In this sense, some indications of our promiscuity, overindulgence, and consumptiveness are more "moral" than they first appear. We buy expensive cars or drift from person to person, not because we are just immoral, but rather because somewhere within us we are desperate for meaning.

The Christian claim is that Jesus Christ, and only Jesus Christ, enables us to make sense of ourselves. By becoming attached to Christ, in having our lives caught up in his work, our lives are given significance. We become fellow workers with him. Our lives take on new meaning since we are now about work which is more important than momentary desires. I am freed from the deadly necessity of having to please everyone, having to create some self-derived significance for my little life, because my life has been subsumed in his light.

A Princeton sophomore was asked by a reporter about the possibility of the United States intervening in Afghanistan when the Soviets invaded. "There's nothing worth dying for," she replied. Which means that one day she will have the unpleasant task of dying for nothing.

Look, we're all going to die for something. Wouldn't it be good to die for what is true, to expend my life for something more significant than a mortgage and a desk in the front office?

"Our people die well," bragged Wesley. That is, Wesley's people had something worthwhile, something worthy to die for: Christian truth.

A disciple is a person of discipline because the disciple has as a life project nothing less than imitation of the master. As Augustine said, "We imitate whom we adore." Any practical, daily disciplines we Christians employ—prayer, Bible reading, small group study, devotional reading, working at the soup kitchen, going to church meetings—are our means of being more adoring of and therefore more faithful to the one who reached out to us and said, "Follow me."

To my surprise, I meet many people today who are hungry for discipline. They have discovered that freedom *from* is not nearly so interesting as freedom *for*. Realizing that life (despite all our mechanisms for avoidance), whether it is lived well or poorly, eventually costs everything they've got, they decide it is better to expend one's life for something that's worthy rather than worthless. Sick of wandering about without chart or compass, without guide or goal, they hunger for form, structure, direction in life. I want to say to them, if they happen to show up at a United Methodist church, "Congratulations, you've come to the right place."

Where I work, as you can imagine, I spend a good deal of time talking to young adults who are planning on marriage. When a couple comes to me to talk about marriage, I sometimes ask them, just to get things rolling, if they are already living together. Many of them are honest enough to admit that they are.

"So why in the world would you want to get married?" I ask. "You're already having sex, doing the dishes together, sharing groceries, toothpaste. What on earth could I or the church give you that you don't already have?"

In their response, they invariably use words like, "We're looking for a more long-term commitment." To which I say, "Congratulations! You've come to the right place. We're in the long-term commitment business. At last you're ready for a promise. That's marriage."

Frustrated by their inability to sustain a relationship with God by purely spontaneous feelings, embarrassed by the superficiality of their lives, many people today are reaching out for the structures of commitment. That's called *discipline.* They've come to the right place when they walk in to the church.

Rather than reducing our life together in the church to the lowest common denominator (a life-style indistinguishable from that followed by everybody else, even those who aren't following Jesus) I believe that we ought to ask more of our people rather than less, ought to build congregations that test the limits of our faithfulness, which expose us to ever deepening dimensions of commitment. The future belongs to churches which create the communal structures and the forms of congregating which are able to sustain discipleship in an unbelieving world.

A while back I met a man on our campus who announced to me that he was a Mormon.

"Just been a Mormon for a few years," he said. "We Mormons really believe a lot of strange things."

"I might have said that," I replied, "but it surprises me to hear *you* say that about your church. What made you a Mormon?"

Without hesitation, he replied, "I love my family."

Then he explained to me how he was "just an average person" who feared that he lacked the personal and moral resources to fulfill his marital responsibilities without help. Now, since his family became affiliated with the Latter Day Saints, he is in church most nights of the week, has had his social life rearranged by the church, and is totally engaged in church work in his spare time. His family is thriving and together—unlike the majority of the families in his neighborhood.

There was a day when that same conversation could have been had by substituting the name "Methodist" for "Mormon."

In his moving *Autobiography*, Malcolm X tells of his conversion to Islam. He was in jail at the time, the place where he had spent much of his adult life. One day, Malcolm received a note from his brother which said only:

DEAR MALCOLM,
    DON'T EAT ANY MORE PORK . . . I'LL SHOW YOU HOW TO GET OUT OF PRISON.

That was all. Don't eat pork? Malcolm said that to him, as a black man, such abstinence was unthinkable, a denial of his whole culture, his whole way of life, a strange turning away from everything that had characterized him up to that point. He had never said no to pork or anything else.

That night, as he went through the line at the prison

cafeteria, Malcolm looked at the food being slopped on the aluminum trays and asked what it was.

"Pork," replied the prison cook.

Malcolm straightened himself and said, "I don't eat pork."

What?

The day that Malcolm said, "I don't eat pork" was a day of rebirth, conversion, empowerment for him. For the first time in his life he was on the road to true freedom by the simple little discipline of saying, "I don't eat pork." Later, he became the national leader of the Black Muslims. (*The Autobiography of Malcolm X* [New York: Grove Press, 1964], pp. 155-56)

John Wesley took ordinary people and gave them a vision of whom they were called to be. But he gave not only a vision. He issued an invitation for them to come out of the cultural status quo of eighteenth-century England, to cast off the chains which enslaved them, and to allow their lives to be disciplined to the way of the cross, promising them that they really could become better people, they really could fashion lives of courage and hope.

So Wesley demanded that all theology, all hymnody, all church structure, all preaching, and all teaching have discipline as their function, the making of disciples. He therefore examined candidates for the Methodist ministry by asking not only about their talents—*Do they know God? Have they received gifts? Have they received graces?*—but also about the practical results of their work—*Have they produced fruit? Are any truly convinced of sin and converted to God by their preaching?*

Forgive us if we United Methodists tend to be a bit busy, tend to be hung up on reports, statistics, record keeping and report reading, tend to be less impressed by the beauty of the music than the numbers of people singing the music, tend to care as much for the varying ethnic colors composing the congregation as for the number within the congregation, tend to judge theology by what it enables us to do more than what it simply asserts as true. Forgive us; sometimes we are practical to a fault. It's one of our unique Wesleyan contributions to the holy catholic church. In fact, if the church is best thought of (according to Paul) as the Body of Christ, then when labeling the anatomy of the Body, we United Methodists wouldn't mind being called Jesus' hands and feet. Not among the most exotic or beautiful parts of the body, I'll grant you, but among the most *practical.*

One of our favorite Charles Wesley hymns stresses this need for disciplined, intentional discipleship:

A charge to keep I have, a God to glorify,
a never-dying soul to save, and fit it for the sky.

To serve the present age, my calling to fulfill;
O may it all my powers engage to do my Master's will!

The great Wesleyan genius was to devise means of disciplining eighteenth-century disciples to "serve the present age." Our challenge, as twentieth- and twenty-first-century followers of Jesus is to *discover* the means of *discipline for disciples* in our age.

When all is said and done, what is the point of the Christian religion? What is the point of discipleship? Jesus told a story about a father and his two sons (Matt. 21:28-32). One day the father asked his boys to go out and work in the field. One son, a dutiful, cooperative, pleasant lad, said, "Yes dear father. I'll be delighted to go to the field and work." An hour later, the boy was still lounging on the living room sofa. The second son, an often disagreeable, surly, contentious boy, replied, "No! I've got better things to do than to slosh around in the muck on a Saturday." That afternoon, the father looked up from his desk and saw, to his delighted surprise, out in the field, his second son bent over, hard at work in the field. Jesus says, "Think hard, class. Which boy did the will of the father? The one who *talked* a good line, or the one who put on his boots and got to work?" I suppose that even someone as dense as Simon Peter got the point, the very *practical* point.

CHAPTER FOUR

BECAUSE CHRISTIANS ARE TO WORSHIP

We United Methodists are practical, busy, energetic people. As I've noted in the previous chapter, we believe that faith should be put into action and that our religion has practical consequences for daily life and society.

But the Rotary also does good for the community, the Men's Garden Club plants petunias, making the town look better, the Wednesday Evening Book Club expands minds, and Scouts gives the kids something wholesome to do in the afternoon.

So what does the church do (The United Methodist Church or any other) that no other organization can do? *We worship God*, that's what. The church exists for no better reason than for listening to, singing songs for, bathing (baptism) in behalf of, eating and drinking (the Lord's Supper) to the glory of, and gathering together for God. The church exists to worship a God who, according to the Bible, loves to be listened to, prayed to, sung for, and glorified. (Read Psalm 150.)

But what *good* does that do? Does Sunday worship put food in hungry mouths, establish a more just society, cure illness, or soothe pain? Well, yes, in a way. But mostly Sunday prayer and praise brings us together with God. Sometimes, in our worship, we are motivated to change our life-style. Sometimes, after the sermon, we are filled with motivation to go out into the world and do justice. Often, through the music, we do feel a sense of great peace and reassurance. But mostly what we get is

God. All of this worthwhile service in our world is but a by-product of the main event of the service of God. We are here on Sunday because we are in love with God. Like all lovers, we overflow with a desire to return some of the love and affection which God has turned toward us.

Someone watches two lovers kiss, write poetry for each other, long to be in each other's presence. The observer asks, "What good does that do?" The question suggests that the questioner has never been in love. The antics of lovers make sense (why are we such *sensible* people?) only to those who are in love.

Likewise, our Sunday praying, preaching, singing, confessing, forgiving, baptizing, and praising makes sense (if you really must make sense) only to those who are actually in love. Worship is the way we act out our love. So, in talking about worship, we are talking about that experience which is at the very center of the church, the heart of Christian being.

The simplest definition of a Christian is that a Christian is someone who gathers on Sunday to worship God through the imitation of Christ. Of course, Christians do much more than gather on Sunday. We also have our Monday through Saturday lives as well. But even there, even in the everyday, workaday, ordinary world on Monday through Saturday, the work we do in the world is close to the work we render in worship. All our being and doing is to the glory of God. When we are at our Christian best, all of our activity, is worship. We praise God on Sundays in the eager expectation that, if we get good enough at it in church, we will also praise God on Monday morning at the office, or at school, or over the kitchen sink, or wherever we find ourselves.

So Christians are none other than those who worship God in Christ.

When United Methodists gather for worship—about three and a half million of us on a typical Sunday morning—our church is at its best. We are at our best in the sense that in worship, Christ is most visibly present among us. When even two or three are gathered, the Risen Christ is there. We are also at our best in the sense that in worship, the unique blending of perspectives and traditions which United Methodism comprises, is often most visibly present. Just as John and Charles Wesley took their Anglican and Catholic love of the sacraments, the noble liturgy of the Western church and combined it with the warm-hearted experience and vibrant preaching of the Wesleyan revival, so our worship blends the best of both worlds of worship—the Catholic (the sacramental worship of the universal church through the ages) and the evangelical (worship through revivalism, hymns, altar calls, testimonials, and biblical preaching for decision).

To those in less expansively minded or less richly traditioned churches the way we United Methodists praise God may seem a bit confused, or even contradictory. But it works for us. When I asked a Roman Catholic friend what he liked about the way we Wesleyans worship, he said, "The warmth, the wonderful warmth!" Later, I asked a Southern Baptist how she liked our Sunday service and she replied, "I love the beautiful liturgy, the way you are dignified without being stuffy, theologically sound without being boringly intellectual." Each was appreciating a different side of our bifocal liturgical tradition.

Not long ago, a couple joined our church. She had grown up as a Catholic, he as a Presbyterian. They found our worship to be a wonderful meeting place for their disparate experiences in Christian worship. She liked the ecumenical flavor, the frequent celebration of the Lord's Supper, and our use of the Common Lectionary for preaching. He liked the biblical preaching, the hymns, and the music of the choir. Our blending of worship traditions makes United Methodists uniquely suited to reach out to a wide array of spiritual needs.

AND SING

You will find us singing spirituals, gospel songs, Hispanic hymns and plain song chants (maybe not in the same congregation but all these genres are in our hymnal), celebrating the sacraments of baptism and the Lord's Supper and still emphasizing biblical preaching and altar calls for personal commitment.

Our 1989 *Hymnal* continues a tradition which goes all the way back to the Wesleys. Charles Wesley wrote sixty-five hundred hymns. You will find a number of them still featured in our *Hymnal,* including a number of Wesley's greatest hits like "Jesus, Lover of My Soul," "Love Divine, All Loves Excelling," "A Charge to Keep I Have," "Hark, the Herald Angels Sing," and "O For a Thousand Tongues to Sing" which we United Methodists love to sing at the top of our voices, despite Father John's advice: "do not bawl when singing."

In the nineteenth century, a blind Methodist laywoman, Fanny Crosby of New York, wrote eight thousand gospel hymns which became mainstays of evangelical Christianity. Hymns like "To God Be the Glory," "Jesus Is Tenderly Calling," "I Am Thine, O Lord," "Blessed Assurance, Jesus Is Mine" are among Crosby's greatest.

Georgia Harkness ("Hope of the World") and Gerald Kennedy ("God of Love and God of Power") are among our twentieth-century Methodist hymn writers. British Methodist F. Pratt Green did not begin writing hymns until after he was sixty. His "When in Our Music God Is Glorified" is one of our favorite new hymns:

When in our music God is glorified,
and adoration leaves no room for pride,
it is as though the whole creation cried
Alleluia!

So has the church in liturgy and song,
in faith and love, through centuries of wrong
borne witness to the truth in every tongue,
Alleluia!

The Wesleys edited a hymnal early in the days of their revival. The first book to be published in the American colonies was our hymnal. Some believe the Wesleys reached the common folk of England and its colonies more through their music than by any other means. Charles sometimes even used the tunes of rather bawdy English drinking songs for some of his hymns. "Why should the Devil have all the good tunes?" he asked. I suspect that, if you want to know our United Methodist theology, the real theology for the person in the pew, you should thumb through our *Hymnal.* Most of our really important ideas about God are sung before they are thought, and music unlocks the deepest wellsprings of emotion. My, do we love to sing.

Our singing is both expressive and informative of our experience of God. In our *Hymnal*, we stress this by arranging many of our hymns according to Wesley's *ordo salutis*, his "order of salvation." So we sing of Prevenient, Justifying, and Sanctifying Grace. Theology put to music, dogma as doxology.

If you wonder how Charles could have possibly found the time to write more than six thousand hymns, consider this entry from a letter of June 2, 1743: "Near Ripley, my horse threw me and fell upon me. My companion thought I had broken my neck; but my leg was only bruised, my hand sprained, and my head stunned; which spoiled my making hymns, or thinking at all, till the next day, when the Lord brought us safe to Newcastle" (Gerald Kennedy, *The Marks of a Methodist*, [Nashville: Methodist Evangelistic Materials, 1960] p. 16).

In *Select Hymns* published in 1761, John Wesley gave his people directions for singing. Among them were: "Sing lustily and with a good courage. Beware of singing as if you were half dead or half asleep; but lift up your voice with strength. Be no more afraid of your voice now, nor more ashamed of its being heard, than when you sung the songs of Satan." On the other hand, he advised, "Sing modestly. Do not bawl, so as to be heard above or distinct from the rest of the congregation, that you may not destroy the harmony; but strive to unite your voices together, so as to make one clear melodious song." (See p. vii of the *United Methodist Hymnal*, 1989.)

John Wesley would have gagged had he ever heard my Uncle Andrew sing "How Great Thou Art." However, surely Father John would agree that in church music, exuberance sometimes makes up for incompetence.

ORDINARY MEANS OF GRACE

As I said in the first chapter, Wesley was big on grace. God's love is a gift, grace coming to us before we come to God, converting us and saving us because of what God has done in Christ rather than what we do or don't do, sanctifying and perfecting us throughout our lives. All this is a gift. We need not *do* anything in the first place except to respond in our daily lives to the work of God's grace in us.

However, although there is nothing we can do to get right with God, fortunately God does much for us. God gives us present, tangible, visible, and audible assurance of his great grace through worship.

Wesley thought that the most important things in the Christian life were too important to be left up to chance or spontaneous feeling. Therefore he stressed the need for prayer, Christian small-group support, Bible reading, attendance at church, and attention to the preached word as well as frequent participation in the Lord's Supper. He defined all of these as "ordinary means of grace." That is, they are the usual ways in which God helps people in the spiritual pilgrimage.

We need not sit back and wait upon the spirit to move us, or until we feel in an appropriately religious mood. Knowing how notoriously fickle are mere feelings, God graciously ordained "ordinary means of grace," through the worship of the church, to sustain us on our way back to God. By "ordinary" Wesley meant not only orderly—systematic, methodical, structured, embodied, and all those other good Wesleyan virtues—but also "ordinary" in the sense of not extraordinary, not spectacular, not special, not weird. If we would like to be with God we need not cool our heels waiting to be zapped by some heaven-sent spiritual laser beam, a message in neon across the evening sky, or divine voices emanating from our refrigerator. Sure, God *could* speak through such extraordinary means like those that make the front page of *The National Enquirer.* But God more usually speaks by the utterly ordinary (and therefore even more gracious) means of preaching, the Lord's Supper, Baptism, Bible reading, and prayer, which are so ordinary that they don't even make the *The United Methodist Reporter.*

So Wesley had little patience with those who whined about the absence or silence of God in their lives because he was convinced that if they were present and speaking to God, God would assuredly be there for them. Did not Jesus promise to show up as long as "two or three are gathered"?

The love of a man and woman is beautiful if it is the

love which sweeps them away into heights of ecstasy and delight, if eyes meet across a crowded room and it's love on sight and you hear Montovani's music the moment you hold hands. But, from a Christian point of view, the best love between a man and a woman is that of the marital variety, the less spectacular, but no less fulfilling love that endures over time, shares burdens, keeps communicating even when it doesn't feel like it, shares doing the dishes and the diapers, in short, love which is utterly *ordinary.*

So don't knock the ordinary—particularly the ordinary, every Sunday *discipline* of putting yourself in the right place at the right time, of listening to sermons, participating in Holy Communion, presenting your child for baptism, confessing sin and receiving forgiveness, and putting your money in the plate when it's passed. Through such ordinary graciousness, God gets to us.

"And they devoted themselves to the apostles' teaching and fellowship, to the breaking of bread and the prayers" (Acts 2:42).

This emphasis on the "ordinary means of grace" accounts for our stress upon *preaching and the sacraments.* It is estimated that John Wesley traveled between three thousand and forty-five hundred miles each year (on horseback) and preached at least two sermons every day from 1748 to 1790 for a total of about forty thousand sermons. His was preaching directed toward decision in his listeners. He wasn't just imparting interesting religious information. Wesley wanted response, commitment, changed lives as a result of his preaching. United Methodist preaching today, at its best, is preaching that hopes to elicit response in its hearers.

Wesley's sermons were well crafted and thoughtful. Yet he also sought to communicate through "plain words to plain people." If you read his *Sermons* today, you may wonder why thousands flocked to hear him. What we have left of his sermons are mostly transcriptions by one of his assistants which undoubtedly lack some of the color and fire of the originals.

Nonetheless, some of the church's greatest preachers have come from the "people called Methodists." Wesley associate George Whitefield was said (by none other than deistic Benjamin Franklin) to be able to move a crowd to tears by the mere mention of the word "Mesopotamia." In the twentieth century, Ralph Sockman and Halford Luccock reached thousands in their radio sermons and books on preaching. British Methodist Leslie Weatherhead enthralled crowds with his intellectually honest, invigorating sermons in London. California Bishop Gerald Kennedy spread the lively word throughout the nation. Georgia Harkness continued the Wesleyan tradition of making complex theological ideas accessible to people through her communicative gifts.

The list goes on, and continues even today. When it comes to preaching the Word, telling the Story in a way which is clear, engaging and evocative of response, we United Methodists immodestly consider ourselves and our preachers to be among the best.

Not everyone has approved of the emotion and vitality of Methodist preaching. Jonathan Swift, author of *Gulliver's Travels*, was a contemporary of Wesley. Just two years after Wesley's Aldersgate experience, Swift made fun of shouting Methodists by describing their worship: "They violently strain their eyeballs inward, half closing the lids; then, as they sit, they are in a perpetual motion of feefaw, making long hums at proper periods, and continuing the sound at equal height; choosing their time in those intermissions while the preacher is at ebb" (W. Garrison and J. K. Bergland, *Strangely Warm* [Nashville: Graded Press, 1971], p. 39).

Wedded to this stress on preaching is our love of the sacraments. At the Lord's Table or before the baptismal font, the word of God is made visible, enacted, and experienced in a way which is tangible, communal, and deeply engaging of all our senses. So Wesley urged his people to enjoy "constant communion" at the Lord's Supper. In fact, a major reason why Methodism eventually became a new church was that a shortage of Anglican clergy meant early American Methodists were unable to receive the sacraments. The Wesleyan revival was, in great part, a sacramental revival, and Methodist converts had an intense desire to demonstrate their new relationship with God by frequent and committed participation in the Lord's Supper. Wesley stressed that this holy meal was not only a "supper for the Saints" (those who had already experienced the love of God working in their lives), but also a "converting ordinance" (a means whereby someone experiences God's love as if for the first time, in an intense and personally transforming way). The Lord's Supper was an evangelical, or a Good News, experience of God's grace.

As Charles' hymn "Come, Sinners to the Gospel Feast" put it:

> Come, sinners, to the gospel feast;
> Let every soul be Jesus' guest.
> Ye need not one be left behind,
> For God hath bidden all humankind.

When nineteenth-century Methodists became concerned about the evils of beverage alcohol, the use of wine at Holy Communion was questioned. A Methodist in New York named Welch provided the solution by pasteurizing and bottling his "Methodist Unfermented Communion Wine." The rest is history.

Like other Christian churches, United Methodists initiate new members through the sacrament of baptism.

Even as the Lord's Supper means everything that eating together means (fellowship, communion, grace, sustenance), so baptism means everything that water means (refreshment, birth, life, death, cleansing). Like the majority of other churches, we baptize the children of parents who are members. As we noted earlier, we follow Wesley's teaching that people are not Christians simply by their doing what comes naturally. We must be converted, born again into the faith. Baptism is a sign of the radical change required to be a Christian. By administering this sacrament at any age during a person's life, we also demonstrate that God's grace is available to anyone at any time in life.

We baptize and administer water by three means: sprinkling (symbolic of the biblical act of sprinkling to cleanse), pouring (symbolic of the pouring out of the Holy Spirit on all people after Pentecost), and immersion (symbolic of our dying and rising with Christ to be new people). Through periodic renewals of our baptismal vows, we continue to testify that God's grace continues to operate within us throughout our lives.

Look in the back of our *Hymnal* and you will see sacramental services which combine the biblical story, the best ecumenical consensus on worship, and traditional United Methodist warmth and simplicity. These services are recommended for United Methodist congregations, though not prescribed. While our church provides model services and worship materials, each United Methodist congregation is free to adapt these resources to its own distinctive expression of faith.

So I've seen Hawaiian United Methodists singing in Tongan, swaying in delight. I've seen Black United Methodists in Boston shouting "Amen!" throughout their service. I witnessed liturgically dancing United Methodists in Los Angeles leaping in leotards. I've watched Korean United Methodists in Kentucky praying in their native tongue. And, last Sunday, I sat with awfully conservative, utterly serious United Methodists here in North Carolina. All, I tell you, are living proof that God really does meet us through myriad ordinary means. We have been given an infinite variety of gifts for praising God, and even today, where two or three of us United Methodists gather, there is not only a probable difference of opinion and a potential committee, but also the presence of Christ, risen and revealed among those whom he has called to worship and witness through a church called United Methodist.

CHAPTER FIVE

BECAUSE CHRISTIANS ARE TO WITNESS

In the late 1890s, a small, soft-voiced woman had just finished a scathing attack on the evils of the beverage alcohol industry. Out of the large audience stepped a very large, visibly angry man, shaking his finger at her and shouting, "You mind your own business!"

The woman faced him, unafraid. "I *am* minding my own business," she replied calmly but firmly. "Men, women, children are *my* business because they are *God's* business."

The woman was Frances E. Willard, President of the Women's Christian Temperance Union, who eventually became a member of the Hall of Fame in the nation's capitol. Her work captured the attention of the nation, and her organization was the first, and by far the largest and the most influential, women's organization in the world at that time.

In 1884, Mary Reed volunteered for missionary work in India. After she had returned to Cincinnati six years later, she happened to notice strange sores on her face and hands. She had contracted the dreaded disease of leprosy. Rather than resign herself to her condition as a curse, she regarded it as a divine call to witness. Mary returned to India where she spent her life ministering to lepers as Director of the Chandag Heights Leper House.

William and Catherine Booth, aflame with concern for the poor and the downtrodden in their mid-nineteenth-century England, walked out of a church meeting, criticizing their church for its sorry "passion for respectability." They went on to found the Salvation Army, which, even today, spans the whole globe with its work on behalf of those whom society has forgotten.

Born in Mayesville, South Carolina, in 1875, Mary McLeod Bethune was the child of former slaves. At age nine, she could pick 250 pounds of cotton per day; however, she could neither read nor write. She was a Methodist, but when the Northern Presbyterian Church opened a school for blacks five miles from her house, Mary enrolled there and studied for ten years. When she later graduated from college, she wanted to be a missionary to Africa. Eventually though, she said, "God made me a missionary to all people of all races in the United States." She founded Bethune-Cookman College in Florida. In 1974, an eighteen-foot bronze statue was erected in her honor in Washington, D.C., the first statue on public ground to honor the memory of either a black person or a woman.

Two common factors unite these diverse people. They were all convinced that the gospel is meant to be shared, in word and deed, in all the world, and they were all heirs of John Wesley and his "people called Methodists."

There are churches which believe that Christians should "stick to saving souls and stay out of politics." We United Methodists are not one of those churches. Not that we take partisan political stands, but rather that we believe that Christ calls us to witness to our faith in every area of our lives. There is no realm of human endeavor—economic, political, sexual, social, educational—which is immune to the light of Christ.

Wesley really expected to change the face of society through his revival. Wesley records that when he began work with the colliers of Kingswood, they were "a people famous . . . for neither fearing God nor regarding man: so against the things of God, that they seemed but one removed from the beasts that perish." But after his revival there, the scene had dramatically changed: "Kingswood does not now, as a year ago, resound with cursing and blasphemy. It is no more filled with drunkenness and uncleanliness and the idle diversions that naturally lead there to. It is no longer full of wars and fightings, of clamour and bitterness, of wrath and envyings. Peace and love are there." (*Journal*, Nov. 27, 1789).

John Wesley set the tone for United Methodist social witness. He always believed that our spiritual commitments have strong implications for our daily lives. In a treatise entitled "The Sermon on the Mount" he summed up his view of a Christian's stewardship of wealth. Wesley believed that those who did not use their money responsibly for God's work "were not only robbing God, continually embezzling and wasting their Lord's goods, but also robbing the poor, hungry, naked; wronging the widow and the fatherless; and making themselves accountable for all the want, affliction and the distress which they made, but do not remove." Strong words indeed, words from a man in whose day poverty was accepted as God's will for the poor or a demonstration that the poor were lazy and did not want to work. When Wesley died, he died in virtual poverty, having given away all his wealth.

He wrote, "I visited many of the poor to see with my own eyes what their wants were and how they might be relieved." When he was accosted by beggars on the streets of London, Wesley always raised his hat to them and willingly gave them alms. True to form, he was an early opponent of the "execrable villainy of slavery." His last letter was one of encouragement to abolitionist William Wilberforce encouraging him in his work. When Wesley died, five poor men bore his body to the grave.

The same concern for those outside the church and

"respectable society" directed Charles Wesley's ministry. One of his hymns proclaims:

> Outcasts of men, to you I call,
>   Harlots and publicans and thieves;
> He spreads his arms to embrace you all,
>   Sinners alone his grace receive,
> No need of him the righteous have,
>   He came the lost to seek and save.

Early in his ministry, John Wesley organized groups of volunteers to visit regularly the sick in London as well as the jails. He gave free medicine to the poor from his house in London, claiming to have given medicine to about 500 persons a week. He even published a book of medical advice for the use of the poor. This was a compilation of simple home remedies for common ailments. (Today, The United Methodist Church has over 80 hospitals in America. We have 64 United Methodist facilities for child care and 214 retirement communities, homes, and nursing homes for the elderly.) Wesley thus demonstrated the biblically sound doctrine that there is no biblical justification for separating spiritual needs from physical ones.

At first, Wesley had said that his mission was only to the "lost sheep" in the Church of England. But a letter from carpenter Thomas Bell convinced Wesley that there were lost sheep aplenty within the wilds of the American colonies. "They [the lost American sheep] have strayed from England into the wild woods here, and they are running wild after this world. They are drinking their wine in bowls, and are jumping and dancing, and serving the devil, in the groves and under the green trees. Are these lost sheep? And will none of the preachers come here?" (Garrison and Bergland, p. 24). Thus began the Methodist mission to North America.

So it is no accident that the 1908 General Conference of the Methodist Episcopal Church composed a forthright official statement on pressing national social issues. It became our first "Social Creed." This document put the church on record for equal rights and justice for all, the abolition of child labor, and fair hours for working women. The Creed took a stand against poverty and the liquor industry and supported collective bargaining for working people. It also articulated a Christian attitude toward the use of property.

It was New York Methodist pastor Frank Mason North who wrote that great twentieth-century hymn "Where Cross the Crowded Ways of Life." This anthem of the social gospel movement found fertile ground among Methodists in the early part of this century.

> Where cross the crowded ways of life,
> where sound the cries of race and clan,
> above the noise of selfish strife,
> we hear your voice, O Son of man!
>
> O Master, from the mountain side,
> make haste to heal these hearts of pain;
> among these restless throngs abide,
> O tread the city's streets again.

If you look at our *Book of Discipline*, you will see this tradition continuing in our church's statement on issues as diverse as women's rights, abortion, nuclear power, ecology, homosexuality, and birth control. If a person's idea of church is a safe haven, isolated from the tough questions of the day, an island in Never-Never Land where everything is discussed except what really matters in this life, then it's a safe bet that person will not be happy among us United Methodists. While our church does not tell us what to think on every pressing social issue it does give us helpful guidance and encourages research, debate, and prayer over social and political questions.

I once had a man, a retired Army colonel, I believe, inquire about joining our church. The week before he was to join, he telephoned me in an agitated state to tell me that he had just read in the newspaper that the United Methodists were opposed to the military draft. He was furious.

"Why should I join a church which says things that make me mad?" he asked.

"Why indeed?" I said. Then I suggested that, before we went further, he ought to sit down and read our United Methodist Social Principles. He agreed to do so and I gave him a copy.

A week later he called again to say that, whereas he disagreed with the official church statement about the draft, he *really* got burned up over some of the other statements. Then he added, "Even though there are some of the Social Principles that I really like, that's probably not the point. The point is that the church is taking a stand and pushing me to take a stand too, to think and act as a Christian. I want to be part of that kind of gutsy church."

At our best, we really are that kind of church. Please be forewarned, don't come among us if you fear controversy and earnest, sometimes fevered debate. But isn't this really more like the faith that Jesus preached and lived then the Never-Never Land variety? When Jesus encountered human suffering, he didn't just pat hurting people on the head and offer a prayer for them. He reached out, touched and healed them. He didn't respond to empty stomachs by filling hungry people with pious platitudes; he fed them. He didn't bow and scrape before the religious and political establishment of his day; he confronted it, criticizing the way the religious leaders of his day heaped up burdens upon the backs of the common people rather than lift those burdens through mercy and justice (Matt. 23:4-7). Jesus was not put on a cross for saying "Blessed are the lilies."

Wesley took controversy and conflict for granted, as a necessary by-product of confronting people with the truth. His dry wit shines through his comments in his *Journal* on a particularly difficult group of folk at St. Ewe: "I went to St. Ewe. There was much struggling here at first; but the two gentlemen who occasioned it are now removed—one to London, the other into Eternity."

A RAINBOW CHURCH

American Methodism became a church at the Christmas Conference of 1784, which was held at Lovely Lane Chapel in Baltimore. A rule was passed condemning American slavery and forbidding American Methodists to hold slaves. This stance, though at odds with the prevailing sentiment in the young nation, was in accordance with Wesley's own opinions on the matter. In a stirring pamphlet published in 1774, John Wesley had labeled slavery "that execrable villainy." One of the first two American bishops, Thomas Coke, had his life threatened more than once for his attacks on the slave trade. By 1826, blacks constituted 40 percent of the Methodists in the Carolinas and Georgia.

Unfortunately, the rule against slavery was short-lived. The General Conference allowed each Annual Conference to decide on the subject. Gradually, Methodists (particularly in the Southern states) were allowed to hold slaves, although the United Brethren remained steadfast in their opposition to slavery. Eventually, the Methodist Church split into Northern and Southern branches over the issue (1844, reunited in 1939). The Wesleyan Methodist Church was formed (1843) by New England Methodist Orange Scott, who was outraged that Methodists appeared to be compromising on the slavery issue.

At least one, possibly two, blacks participated in the founding Christmas Conference—the famous black preacher Harry Hosier, and Richard Allen. Allen, in response to racial discrimination in the Methodist Episcopal Church, joined with other black leaders to form the African Methodist Episcopal Church, forerunner of the great, predominantly black, Methodist denominations in the U.S.

Today, black United Methodists constitute a significant portion of our church, supplying a disproportionate number of our church's leaders.

Aggressive mission efforts by the Methodists in the late nineteenth and early twentieth centuries made thousands of converts in Asia, Africa, and Latin America. When many of these peoples immigrated to the United States or others were converted by evangelistic efforts here, they gave the United Methodist Church a veritable rainbow of colors, creating one of the largest and most varied ethnic constituencies among American churches. Recently, our church has experienced its most dramatic growth among Hispanic and Korean United Methodists.

A church is known by the people it gathers around the Lord's Table. When we look around and see all the colors of the rainbow, people from every economic class and ethnic origin, we see the best evidence that our church is being obedient to Jesus' command to be witnesses, to "go into all the world and make disciples" (Matt. 28:19).

How bland and uninteresting would be a church where everyone was the same shade of gray rather than part of a rich rainbow of color!

WITNESS IN EDUCATION

There are churches which feel that reason, the use of the mind, and higher education are a threat to faith. For them, Christians are people who swallow as much religion as possible with a minimal number of questions asked. The United Methodist Church is not one of these churches.

Methodists have always emphasized education, an interest which certainly stemmed from our founder's own commitments. Wesley earned the equivalent of a Ph.D. while attending Oxford. He was fluent in Greek, Latin, Hebrew, and Arabic. He had expertise in the languages of the Bible and loved to read ancient, classical literature which he freely quoted throughout his life. He wrote notes on Shakespeare's plays and knew reams of Milton by heart as well as the more recent poets of the eighteenth century like Alexander Pope. He studied medicine and loved to shower medical advice on his friends. He told his preachers to "read, read, read."

No sooner had Methodists built a few churches in the new United States than they began building schools. I am the product of both Wofford College and Emory University and teach and preach at Duke University which are among our one hundred and four colleges and universities in thirty-eight states and the District of Columbia. We also have nine secondary schools and one elementary school along with thirteen seminaries and schools of theology.

From the first days of the movement, while still under the hand of Wesley, our preachers were expected to have rigorous preparation and training. One of Charles Wesley's hymns speaks of the desire to "unite the two so long disjoined, knowledge and vital piety." That is just what the Wesleys did in their own lives and encouraged in the lives of their followers—the linking of learning with experienced, living faith. We have always felt that true faith is not weakened by clear thinking; it is strengthened. So as soon as the Methodists had cleared a path in the wilds of North Carolina, they joined the Quakers to found a little college called Trinity. Then, when Southern Methodist James B. Duke left his fortune to make a university out of Trinity that would eventually bear his name, it was only natural that its motto should be "Religion and Learning."

Earlier, one of Trinity's professors, Dr. Bassett, was viciously attacked for publishing an article which argued for racial justice in the American South, a huge public outcry demanded his removal from Trinity. How dare someone stir up controversy—and at a *church* school? Trinity was a *Methodist* church school, the college of a church which was not threatened by reason and the exercise of the mind. Dr. Bassett stayed at Trinity, and thereby set the tone for academic freedom at other American institutions of higher education.

Methodist preacher and popular historian Halford Luccock once said that, whereas Martin Luther claimed to have thrown his ink bottle at the devil, John Wesley hurled an entire printing press at him—writing 440 books, tracts, and pamphlets. Francis Asbury, first American Methodist bishop, said that the religious press "is next in importance to the preaching of the Gospel." Four weeks after George Washington became President of the United States, the Methodist publishing house was founded (May 28, 1789). John Wesley earned and gave away $150,000 through his publishing efforts (equivalent to several million dollars today). The United Methodist Publishing House publishes over 150 million items each year (like this book you are reading) in addition to its thousands of curriculum and church school materials. And you can find one of our Cokesbury Bookstores in most of the nation's major cities. For what it's worth, you may be glad to know that publications from our United Methodist Publishing House now require about 130 tons of ink per year.

In the late 1700s, Hannah Ball, member of the Methodist Society at High Wycombe, England, began a Sunday school for children. United Methodist churches continue this great tradition of lay education in our churches. Over four million of our members participate in Sunday school programs in their churches as well as in the extensive study programs sponsored by the United Methodist Women and other informal educational experiences. Many persons are first attracted to a United Methodist congregation through a church school class.

In a sometimes confusing, disordered, challenging world, where ordinary folk like you and I are trying to live our faith, it is important for us to think about the Christian faith and how it impacts our daily lives. Through the many facets of the educational ministry of our church, we are given an opportunity to grow in our faith, to embody that good old Wesleyan process of "growth in grace," sanctification. We reflect upon our values, weigh our commitments, deepen our comprehension of scripture, and thus become better equipped and more mature Christians. We thereby witness to the truth that, to be a believer in Christ, one need not let tough, intelligent questions go begging, one need not close one's mind or escape the realities of the modern world. Thus, the educational emphasis of United Methodism is a witness to the vitality of being a Christian in our time and place.

GOOD NEWS TO THE POOR

By no mere coincidence did Wesley take as the text for his first attempt at field preaching, Jesus' first sermon at his hometown synagogue in Nazareth (Luke 4). "The Spirit of the Lord is upon me to preach *good news to the poor.*"

Aldersgate inflamed Wesley's heart to spread the good news of Christ to everyone, everywhere, particularly to those who felt alienated from the ministrations of the established church. When that meant communicating the gospel in "plain words for plain people," Wesley gladly did so. When that meant developing new structures to bring help to the sick, the poor, the uneducated,and the addicted, Wesley creatively designed such structures.

The historian Sir Herbert Butterfield noted that, for the most part, Wesley's work was among "the most brutalized section of the population." Wesley was disturbed by bleak poverty and felt that Methodists were called to personal and institutional reforms which would aid the poor. He instituted educational and economic opportunity programs. He defended those who opposed slavery. He felt that the poor had a particular claim upon the gospel and, for the most part, did not seek out or attempt to evangelize the upper classes. Wesley did not establish a single Methodist preaching post in any of the five wealthier boroughs of London.

On May 21, 1771, Wesley preached from Hebrews 8:10-12, which reads, "For all shall know me from the least to the greatest." He noted that God's way seems to begin with the "least of these" before moving on to the greatest. He used the Methodist movement as an example of how God begins with those whom the world regards as lowly and of little account before God tries much with the rich and the powerful. Wesley lived in an England where the poor suffered terribly. In response, Wesley not only preached to the poor, but he also arranged for interest-free loans to the needy through a lending society, instituted relief work for the unem-

ployed, and even established a clothes-making cooperative for unemployed women. Disgusted by the lack of
medical services for the poor, in 1746 he organized
volunteers to visit the sick in assigned districts and
wrote health pamphlets and his *Primitive Physic*, the
book of inexpensive home remedies for the sick.

He showed amazing understanding of the systemic
causes of poverty in his day. Wesley urged Methodist
women to wear no jewels, hair curling, velvets or silks.
Money should be given to the poor rather than spent on
such superfluous finery. He was even-handed in his
advice to Methodist men, telling them to forgo fashion-
able stockings, costly buckles, and wigs. He even told
Methodists to stay away from expensive, smoked, and
highly spiced foods because they were more costly than
nourishing.

He practiced what he preached—fasting regularly,
preferring inexpensive herbal tea to imported tea. When
he computed how much he spent in one year going (even
infrequently) to the barber, he determined to cut his own
hair and give the money saved to the poor.

Growing prosperity among the once poor Methodists
was a source of pride to Wesley, but much more a source
of great concern.

> Wherever riches have increased, the essence of religion
> has decreased in the same proportion. Therefore I do not
> see how it is possible in the nature of things for any
> revival of religion to continue long. For religion must
> necessarily produce both industry and frugality, and
> these cannot but produce riches. But as riches increase so
> will pride, anger, and love of the world in all its branches.
> How then is it possible that Methodism, that is, a religion
> of the heart, though it now flourishes as a green bay tree,
> should continue in this state? For the Methodists in every
> place grow diligent and frugal; consequently they

increase in goods. Hence they proportionately increase in pride, anger, in the desire of the eyes and the pride of life. So, although the form of religion remains, the spirit is swiftly vanishing away. (D. E. Loder, ed., *The People Called Methodist*, [Nashville: Discipleship Resources, 1984] p. 38)

In economic matters, Wesley's directions to his followers were typically terse and to the point: "Make all you can; save all you can; give all you can." One wonders if latter-day United Methodists have kept the emphasis on the last Wesleyan admonition to be as good at giving as we are at getting.

The Wesleyan penchant for bringing the gospel, in word and deed, to every class of society, led the stuffy Duchess of Buckingham to comment to Lady Huntington:

Their doctrines are most repulsive and tinctured with impertinence and disrespect toward their superiors, perpetually endeavoring to level all ranks and doing away with all distinctions. It is monstrous to be told that you have a heart as sinful as the common wretches that crawl the earth. This is highly offensive and insulting. (A. C. H. Seymour, *Life and Times of Huntington*, vol. I, 1840, p. 27)

Then, as now, it takes courage to be a witness. Powerful forces urge conformity to the status quo and adherence to conventional, merely socially approved standards of behavior. Yet wherever the gospel is preached or enacted, it has always produced a collision with conventional values. Thus we need a church so confident of its vision, so determined to be faithful to Christ at all cost, so equipped to put loyalty to the Good News above all other loyalties that ordinary people will be empowered to be anything but ordinary witnesses.

When he ordained one of his deacons (May 20, 1815) tough old Bishop Francis Asbury prayed, "O Lord, grant that these brethren may never want to be like other people." At our best, that has been a typically United Methodist prayer, a prayer for the grace never to be just like everybody else.

John Wesley worried that he had become respectable in the last years of his life. He wrote to Elizabeth Ritchie that he had become, to his great displeasure, "an honorable man." As Wesley saw it, "The scandal of the cross is ceased; and in all the kingdom, rich and poor, Papist and Protestants behave with courtesy, nay, and seeming good will! It seems as if I had well nigh finished my course, and the Lord was giving me an honorable discharge" (*The Letters of the Rev. John Wesley, A.M.,* John Telford, ed., [London: The Epworth Press, 1931] vol. I, p. 277).

As you enter the university chapel where I preach, you must first pass through a wonderfully carved limestone arch over the front door. There, staring down in dignity, are assorted heroes, saints of the faith. They serve as reminders of the cost of discipleship. There is Martin Luther, the Florentine friar Savonarolla, Bible translator Wycliff, all presided over by John Wesley and the first bishops of American Methodism, Thomas Coke and Francis Asbury. (My Lutheran friends express befuddlement over why Wesley, Asbury, and Coke stand higher than Martin Luther. I tell them that the reason is simple and non-theological—Methodists paid for the chapel.) Although gathered from diverse times and places in the church's life, these now silent, still, staring witnesses are united by one factor: *all of them* were troublemakers, disturbers of the peaceful status quo.

More than one was burned at the stake. (In the Bible, the word which we translate as "witness" is also the root for the word "martyr".) All of them suffered public disapproval but dared to swim against the stream. I can think of no better way to welcome people into the church than with these visible reminders of the potential cost of discipleship. They stand there as a silent but eloquent rebuke whenever church people, in Francis Asbury's words, try to be "like other people," or when United Methodists degenerate into merely "honorable" people. Every time we enter the church, we take our place in that glorious procession of misfits, troublemakers, protestors, and saints.

When visiting local Methodist Societies, Wesley often asked a question which, if answered wrong, could send their preacher packing off to another place: Who has your preacher made angry this past year? Of this possibility, Wesley had warned his preachers. He said that the life of a Circuit Rider was not "the way to ease, honour, pleasure or profit. It is a life of much labor and reproach." We are "liable to be beaten, stoned, and abused in various manners. Consider this, before you engage in so uncomfortable a way of life."

When Jacob Albright (co-founder with Martin Boehm and Philip W. Otterbein of the Evangelical United Brethren Church), preached the need for a change of heart as a test of true religion, mobs in Pennsylvania, Maryland, and Virginia beat him severely. Methodist and E.U.B., united two churches with histories of challenging comfortable Christianity.

Is that why we love to sing Bishop Gerald Kennedy's rousing hymn, "God of Love and God of Power"?

> God of love and God power,
> grant us in this burning hour
> grace to ask these gifts of thee,
> daring hearts and spirits free.
>
> We are not the first to be
> banished by our fears from thee;

> give us courage, let us hear
> heaven's trumpets ringing clear.
> God of Love and God of power,
> thou has called us for this hour.

Sometime ago, I was in a church meeting where the group was discussing a trip to our state capital to protest our state's use of the death penalty. A number of persons in the group expressed reservations about the church involving itself in such controversy.

A woman stood and said, in a strong, clear voice: "We're United Methodists, for heaven's sake! This is our church at its best." For heaven's sake, indeed.

So we use that word *witness* in a twofold sense. To witness means to have seen and heard something. To witness also means to testify to having seen and heard something. United Methodists, following in the train of John Wesley, Frances E. Willard, William and Catherine Booth, and Mary McLeod Bethune have witnessed the advent of God into human history in Christ, witnessed the power of God doing good things for the poor and the imprisoned. Therefore we witness to the world—in word and deed, personally and institutionally, individually and collectively, spiritually and materially—to the love of God in Christ.

We are United Methodists, for heaven's sake, as well as for the sake of our parish, the whole wide world.

CHAPTER SIX

BECAUSE CHRISTIANS ARE TO GROW

The word "theology" has a dry academic, forbidding sound to the ears of many people. Theology sounds like some arcane, esoteric endeavor. Sometimes, that's what we have reduced theology to—something for a Ph.D. dissertation but not anything related to real life. Theology in this sense is not a United Methodist interest. Theology is not only an endeavor to *talk about God*, but also an attempt to *live with God*. Theology is not simply an exercise in intellectual reflection upon the ideas of Jesus, but also our effort to put the way of Jesus into practice. Tom Langford says that, for Wesley:

> Theology is never an end, but is always a means for understanding and developing transformed living. There was little speculative interest involved in Wesley's theological investigations. He consistently turned theological reflection to practical service. Theology, in his understanding, was to be preached, sung, and lived. (*Practical Theology* , pp. 20-21)

Sometimes we United Methodists have been criticized as having no theology. I am tempted to get defensive and talk about what a marvelous and creative theologian Wesley was, or cite some of our great theological thinkers of the past or present. However, the person making such a charge may have, from our point of view, too limited a notion of theology. If we mean that every

United Methodist could construct a systematic theological statement, or affirm a binding confession of faith, then our theological ability seems rather lean. However, if one uses the term *theology* in a dynamic sense to mean that someone senses the grace of God in his or her life and shows forth the results of that grace, then the United Methodist Church is chock full of theology. While our theology may not be sophisticated, it is able to articulate the Good News of Christ in a way that changes lives; it also puts great stress on reaching out to those in need in specific ways. Our theology may not be recited in a catechism, but it can be expressed in love and care for one another. United Methodism is a large and diverse group of people who have come forth to worship and to serve a very personal Savior. That commitment to God means that we firmly believe that no one is excluded from the grace of God by virtue of age, sex, race, or any other means whereby the world draws boundaries between people.

Wesley called his theology, as embodied in his hymns and sermons, "practical divinity"—that is, thoughts about God which are meant to be put into practice. We have no interest in sitting back, coolly discussing long thoughts about deep subjects ("speculative" theology, Wesley called it). We want to see God-talk transformed into God-walk, daily (Wesley loved that word), ordinary, practical (two more good Wesleyan words) embodiment of our beliefs in our lives.

I have sometimes envied the theological certainty which members of some other denominations seem to have. For instance, I know Lutherans who know what truly *Lutheran* theology is. Most United Methodists don't enjoy this luxury. When we think about God, we sometimes appear to roam all over the theological landscape. Part of our apparent theological uncertainty is our theological richness. When we drink at the waters of theology, we are refreshed by water which has flowed from many different sources.

From the time he was ordained, John Wesley was a priest in the *Church of England.* He loved this church and saw his Methodist movement as an attempt to reform the Church of England from the inside. Wesley particularly loved the Anglican *Book of Common Prayer.* When American Methodists asked him for directions in worship, Wesley merely sent them his abridged version of the *Book of Common Prayer* and insisted that they adhere to the Anglican Articles of Religion. In his Church of England, Wesley found what was to him "true, scriptural Christianity."

Anglican theology always emphasized acts of devotion such as the sacraments. Much of our sanctification emphasis comes from the Anglicans. Some things should not be left up to chance or to our individual, inner feelings. God has ordained certain ordinary means of grace like the Lord's Supper.

From the *Moravians* and other pietists in Germany Wesley eventually obtained his emphasis on instantaneous conversion and personal, experienced faith. These German pietists taught Wesley to look for the experience which he eventually had at Aldersgate. When the Methodist Church united with the Evangelical United Brethren Church in 1968, the Methodists were joined to a family of German-rooted churches which had always laid great stress on the personal, evangelical experience of faith, an experience begun in Wesley (with help from the Moravians) and continued in leaders like Otterbein, Boehm, and Albright.

Yet another stream flowing into the river of Wesleyan theology was *Puritanism.* Puritanism had been an attempt to reform Anglicanism. Puritanism stressed the need to view the church and its theology in a critical way, to be suspicious of established, too formalized religious practices which followed the letter of the law rather than the spirit. The Puritan tradition also led Wesley to stress the need for a covenant people, a visible gathering of people bound together for mutual support and correction.

United Methodists have always been influenced by the social context out of which our movement grew. Eighteenth-century England was, like our own age, a time of great social problems. Even as drug addiction is a tragic problem in our own day, alcohol addiction was a major social disease in Wesley's day. He set the tone for us in his courageous attack on the alcohol trade and other social evils. Wesley always maintained a connection between personal and social holiness, believing that the church was a means of reforming the whole society.

Wesley found, early on, that it is tough for a church to exist as an alternative to the status quo in the surrounding society. Members realize that they must embrace society's values in order to be accepted and to prosper—as that society defines prosperity. Wesley therefore devised a church structure which provided eighteenth-century England with a distinctive alternative and enabled ordinary, poor English people to rise above their miserable economic conditions.

One of the most distinctive features of Wesley was his linkage, within his own life, of aspects of the "holy living" tradition with his evangelical stress on conversion. Holy living meant offering up one's whole life to God as a living sacrifice, loving God and one's neighbor as completely as possible, and attempting to imitate Christ in our daily lives. Wesley came to view the Christian life as a pilgrimage of personal and social holiness. His organizational structure, the small group societies which he formed, were part of this effort to live a life that was holy in all aspects.

One of John Wesley's favorite books was *The Imitation*

of Christ by Thomas à Kempis. There he read that "high curious reasons make not a man holy nor righteous, but a good life maketh him beloved with God" (Book I). Or, as Wesley himself never tired of saying, Christianity is considerably more than "true opinions." It is a way of life; "holiness of heart and life" said Wesley. In his popular work *The Character of a Methodist,* Wesley advised followers to "be sure of your faith, try it by your living, look upon the fruits." A Methodist is a character who is "inwardly and outwardly conformed to the will of God, as revealed in the written word. . . . He so walks as Christ walked."

One of Wesley's favorite words was "daily." He took very seriously Jesus' call to his disciples to "take up your cross *daily.*" Every moment of our lives, even the apparently insignificant moments, are moments to be walked with God. Every aspect of our lives can be held accountable to God. We never forget that Wesley's faith became real and personal for him when he "attended reluctantly" a rather dull church meeting! That keeps reminding us that God can meet us anywhere, even at church meetings! So we believe that it is important to walk with Christ, to expect to meet Christ as we go about our daily lives.

United Methodist theology continues to be shaped by John Wesley's identity as a "folk theologian." Wesley always asserted that there should be a close link between our knowledge and our piety, what we know of theology and how we enact our theology in everyday life. We think about God in order to serve God better. Truth is sought from a wide range of perspectives, avoiding detached intellectualism on the one hand and shallow sentimentalism on the other. This is a difficult tightrope for us to walk.

So our theology has always been characterized by *eclectic openness.* From Wesley to the present, we have drawn widely on both the Protestant and the Catholic traditions. We find points of agreement and disagreement with every major theological stream. To some, this makes us appear as if we are "blown to and fro by every wind of doctrine." However, at our best, it means that we offer an open hand to our fellow Christians of a wide variety of theological traditions, while still avoiding mushy indifferentism. At times, our eclecticism has caused problems, as we sometimes say of ourselves that "we United Methodists don't know what we believe."

What we believe is that God's truth is rich and diverse, unable to be captured or comprehended through dogmatic narrowness and rigidity. Even as the Bible itself contains a rich panoply of theological perspectives, so our church tries to make room for the great diversity of means by which God is disclosed to people.

WE ARE EVANGELICAL

Another feature of our Wesleyan theological spirit is our *evangelical focus.* The word "evangelical" can mean lots of things. When we use it, we mean the spirit that focuses on faithfulness to the basic and earliest creeds of Christianity as well as the biblical witness, faithfulness felt in joyful, personal experience of living faith. After all, *evangel* means "good news." To hear the good news of Christ is to be filled with joy and to respond in gratitude. To be "evangelical" is to be engaged in that sort of hearing and response. One of our parent bodies was the *Evangelical* United Brethren (E.U.B.).

We United Methodists seek *evangelical results.* That means that we want more than information. We want transformation. Our theology does not exist just to assert abstractly what is true but to *persuade,* to *change* people and society. Wesley abhorred "dead orthodoxy." One of his favorite ways of describing his preaching was, "I offered Christ." This means much more than the conventional definition of "getting saved." It means to expose persons to the warm glow of God's grace and to call them to reflect that grace in all areas of their lives. In other words, our theology seeks visible, experienced evangelistic results in response to the offer of the love of Christ.

Wesley began his work within the confines of the established church. But soon he was preaching on the outside. In fact, some believe that Wesley's willingness "to be more vile" and to engage in the strange practice of open-air field preaching was his *real* conversion experience, even more so than Aldersgate. He writes in his *Journal* on April 2, 1739:

> At four in the afternoon, I submitted to be more vile, and proclaimed in the highways the glad tidings of salvation, speaking from a little eminence in a ground adjoining to the city, to about three hundred thousand people. The Scripture on which I spoke was this (Is it possible any one should be ignorant, that it is fulfilled in every true minister of Christ?) "The Spirit of the Lord is upon me, because he hath anointed me to preach the Gospel to the poor; he hath sent me to heal the brokenhearted; to preach deliverance to the captives, and recovery of sight to the blind; to set at liberty them that are bruised, to proclaim the acceptable year of the Lord."

Our evangelistic vigor accounts for the expansive, constantly growing nature of the worldwide Methodist movement. Just as Wesley went beyond the boundaries of established religion, United Methodism smashed one boundary after another. It smashed the boundary of the limited ecclesiastical parish in England, with Wesley declaring the whole world to be his parish. It smashed the boundary of class, with Wesley preaching grace to all classes of people. It smashed the boundary of tradition, with Wesley devising new approaches to proclaiming the faith by going into the mines, entering the prisons, standing on street corners, and holding forth in open fields. It smashed the boundaries of gender, with Wesley sowing the seeds for the emancipation of women in the church. It smashed the boundaries of poverty and ignorance, with Methodists acting as leaders in bringing education within the reach of all persons.

Evangelical Christians believe that humanity is fallen, that we cannot help or save ourselves by relying only upon ourselves. Therefore, we must reach out to the God who has reached out to us in Christ. My old professor, church historian Sydney Ahlstrom of Yale, argued that American Methodists continued Wesley's evangelical emphasis on the sovereignty of God and the depravity of humanity. No one spoke more forcefully about humanity's abject need for divine grace than Wesley. Our innate sinfulness led to Methodism's demand for complete and thoroughgoing repentance and conversion. This stress upon our sin and our need for conversion accounted for Methodism's moral force on the American frontier, according to Ahlstrom. We didn't accept things as they were. The present social order is the result of human sin rather than divine will. Change was the name of our game.

It is strange that latter-day Methodists should be accused, sometimes justly, of a naïve, too optimistic assessment of human nature. Anyone who seriously confronts injustice and evil in his or her own life or in our society, should be cured of such optimism. Anyone who seeks to reach out in love to the downtrodden within our world should gain a healthy appreciation for human sin and its results. Perhaps Methodism's later unfounded, even un-Wesleyan optimism about the natural human condition is the result of our lack of commitment to and involvement in ministering to those victimized by the social evils of our day. If you view the world from the comfortable vantage point of affluence and power enjoyed by those at the top, the world looks like a rather rosy place and people appear to be basically good. However, if you dare to stand beside those who are on the bottom (the poor, the captives, and the oppressed to whom Wesley preached Good News) you see the sad human wreckage of a fallen and sinful world. Sometimes your theology is a function of where you are standing when you are thinking.

THE FOURFOLD GUIDE FOR BELIEF

As an Anglican, Wesley already knew and used three means of determining appropriate Christian belief: scripture, tradition, and reason. Because of the influences of his own faith journey as well as Puritanism and Moravian thought, he added a fourth test of belief—*experience*. Experience was perhaps the most dangerous and potentially most misunderstood aspect of Wesleyan theology—a matter which Wesley apparently knew because he spent a great deal of effort defending himself against charges of "enthusiasm"—a term of contempt which is somewhat akin to our description of someone as a "fanatic" who has "gone off the deep end."

While it is true that we United Methodists don't insist that you affirm any one of the historic creeds of the Christian faith (note that we list a number of creeds in the back of our *Hymnal* for use in worship) we do *not* mean thereby that as a United Methodist one has a license to believe anything you like. We mean that through the use of our fourfold test, you are given the grace to be a theologian, but a better theologian than you might be if left to your own devices.

Wesley's statement, "If thy heart is right as my heart

is right, give me thy hand," has been mistakenly used to cover thelogical mushiness and contemporary, open-minded pluralism. Wesley was a foe in his day of "speculative and latitudinarian thinking"—folk who were open-minded to a fault. In his great sermon on the "Catholic Spirit" which pleads for Christian charity to be shown by Methodists toward other churches, Wesley definitely advocates something more substantial than open-ended pluralism. He says that a person of "truly Catholic experience . . . is fixed as the sun in his judgment concerning the main branches of Christian doctrine . . . He does not halt between two opinions or vainly try to bring them into one" (*Works*, Abingdon Bicentennial Edition 2:93)

In our theology, we do allow much latitude. However, we also desire to conform our belief in the "main branches of Christian doctrine" and refuse to try to harmonize conflicting beliefs that cannot be brought "into one." All of our theologizing takes place in the context of our "fixed as the sun" confidence in the grace of God as well as the Wesleyan fourfold test for belief—the quadrilateral: scripture, tradition, reason, and experience.

SCRIPTURE

As John Wesley began his search for a relationship with God, he began in Scripture. He said that he studied the Bible because it was "the one, the only standard of truth and the only model of pure religion" (*Works*, Jackson, 2:367). Toward the end of his life he could continue to claim, "My ground is the Bible. . . . I follow it in all things great and small" (ibid., 3:251). In speaking of a fourfold test for belief, it is clear that Wesley set Scripture above tradition, reason, and experience in terms of ultimate authority. (The quadrilateral is not equilateral.)

United Methodists can therefore be said to have a "high" view of scripture. However, we cannot be accused of bibliolatry, inerrancy, literalism, or fundamentalism. Wesley could boast that he was "a man of one book." However, he did not mean this in a naïve, uninformed way. He also meant that he not only *believed* but attempted to *live* by this one book.

TRADITION

We live in an ahistorical time when people are skeptical of guidance from the past. On the other hand, we live in an age when people are hungry for roots and deeper foundations. Wesley, like his beloved Church of England, stressed the need for the church to learn from and to be linked to the past. He was particularly attracted to the church of A.D. 100 to 450—what he called a time of "primitive Christianity." Through our emphasis on tradition, we United Methodists gain perspective, guidance, and discernment in analyzing the signs of our times. History also gives us some humility. We are not the first to struggle to follow Jesus. We don't have to "reinvent the wheel" so far as our spiritual journey is concerned. We can learn from the saints. One reason our *Hymnal* is so big and fat is not only because it was put together by a committee, but also because it includes the diverse products of two thousand years of Christian praise.

REASON

There are churches which feel that use of one's brain is a distinct threat to one's faith. As we said earlier in regard to education, United Methodism is not one of those churches. Wesley frequently spoke of the need for a "reasonable faith." While he knew that reason has its limits and can often be a cover for our own ego, he considered reason a divine gift. "All irrational religion is false religion" (*Letters*, Telford, 5:364). He also admitted the limits of reason. "Reason cannot produce faith in the scriptural sense of the word" (*Works*, Jackson, 6:355). A reasonable, balanced faith cannot be substituted for an engaged and active faith. This kept Wesley from lapsing into the urbane, balanced, but woefully cold faith which bound many intellectuals in his day. Rationalistic Deism conceived a remote God who created, but is now utterly detached from the world. While Wesley's warm faith repudiated Deism, he affirmed that reason enables us to enrich our theology with truth from other fields of human endeavor and scientific disciplines. It keeps our faith applicable to the demands of contemporary life. It subjects our experience, no matter how deeply felt, to the scrutiny of reflection and judgment.

EXPERIENCE

Wesley stressed experience because of his own Aldersgate encounter. "What Christianity (considered as a doctrine) promised is accomplished in my soul" (*Works*, Jackson, 10:75-79). It is, as some have said, the truth made personal.

Wesley felt the need to clarify what he meant by experience, and we should too. We live in a highly privatized, individualized age. When we use the word experience, we do not mean mere subjectivism or libertarianism. Personal religious experience must withstand examination and testing by the other angles of the Wesleyan quadrilateral. When we say experience, we are not merely making a new God of the I and the Me. However, we do mean that personal, undeniable work of the Holy Spirit which enlivens and animates our doctrine.

In a letter to William Law in London on January 6, 1756, Wesley said, "So far as you add philosophy to religion, just so far you spoil it." Philosophy was something you contemplate and discuss. Very objective, very academic and dry. Experienced religion finds its way not only into a person's heart, but also into that person's will. It makes a difference. Warmed hearts produce willing hands.

One early prominent New England Methodist preacher, "Father Taylor," said, "It would take as many of Emerson's dry sermons to convert a man as it would take quarts of skim milk to make him drunk." The preaching of Wesley's heirs, both then and now, has been characterized by its emotional vitality, warmth, and attempt to speak to the head and the heart. As a student once said after one of my sermons (I think meaning a compliment), "You United Methodist preachers always preach to the gut."

Wesley's practical, common sense approach to religion may have been inherited from Peter Bohler, a young Moravian university teacher who, when Wesley was in turmoil before Aldersgate, advised Wesley "to get that philosophy of yours out of your system . . . preach faith till you have it." Sometimes it's possible to *act* as a Christian before you *think* like a Christian.

In my last congregation, I invited all of the doctors and lawyers in the congregation to join me for a six-week exploration of how our Christian faith made a difference in the way we as doctors, lawyers, and a minister, went about our work. Each person presented a case study of the most difficult situation he or she had encountered recently which raised an ethical question. Then we applied the fourfold Wesleyan quadrilateral to each situation, asking ourselves what the Bible, church tradition, our own ability to reason, or our experiences of God had to say about each situation. Of course, use of the fourfold test did not tell us exactly what the "Christian" response to every situation would be, but at least it gave us the theological parameters, pointed us in the right direction, and prodded us to apply standards of more substance than our own personal opinions. The fourfold test is more a compass, pointing us in the right direction, than a detailed road map telling us which step to take next. Still, there's nothing amiss in going in the right direction.

THE SPIRIT OF UNITED METHODIST THEOLOGY

Joy is the hallmark of the Christian life. Wesley hoped to link holiness and happiness. "Sour Godliness is the devil's religion," he once said. Joy is the by-product of our walk with God, a sense that our little lives are part of the larger purposes of God's saving activity in the world. As he lay dying Wesley could rejoice, "The best of all, God is with us."

The story of Jesus begins at Bethlehem (Luke 2) with an outburst of joy because of the advent of Emmanuel—God with us. Salvation is not some momentary occurrence for us, nor is it some sealed-in-concrete state of spiritual smugness. Salvation is a process, a joyful by-product of God being with us.

Although other United Methodists might highlight other aspects of our rich theological legacy, here are three uniquely United Methodists aspects of our godly thought and action:

First, our theology is a *theology of mission.* From one perspective, our theology looks extremely pragmatic. What works is what we believe; we believe what works. Of course, this can be a problem when it degenerates into crude utilitarianism. But at its best, we mean that what we believe should be both motivation and guide for mission. Wesley believed that God raised up Methodism to revive the church and to reform the nation. He used such phrases as "the world is my parish," "faith working in love," "spreading scriptural holiness across the land" to keep reminding his people that they had a mission. Our structure, at its best, is a function of our mission. Our goal is not institutional preservation, the care and feeding of clergy. Our point is not to keep our ecclesiastical machinery well oiled and maintained, as if the machinery itself were more important than its product. We exist for mission.

Our United Methodist pragmatism can be a destructive thing. We ought to make our decisions on the basis of something more than simply what works. However, Wesley's pragmatism points the way for us today. The church is an inherently traditionalist and conserving institution, as are all institutions. Most insitutions, including those which mouth liberal and progressive platitudes, generally protect their life by simply doing what they have always done. Through the use of field preaching, local preachers, small groups, and so forth, Wesley showed that the gospel is to be effective and active. He was an amazingly innovative and creative person, particularly in his creation of new structures which were peculiarly adapted to the needs of people in his day. United Methodists are quite right in assuming that God really is alive and active and means to have an impact on our lives. Mission comes first; institution, second.

When criticized for his use of uneducated lay preachers, Wesley said, "Give me 100 preachers who fear nothing but sin and desire nothing but God, and I care not a straw whether they be clergymen or laymen, such alone will shake the gates of hell and set up the kingdom of heaven upon earth" (*Letters*, Telford, ed., vol. 6, p. 271). God help our church if we lose our once bold determination to change the form of the church to suit the changing mandate of our mission. Mission comes first.

A second emphasis is our *theology of love*. Wesley's choice of Matthew 22:35-40 as a guiding text for Methodism was not accidental. Our church is to be an institutional embodiment of the two great commandments to love God and to love the neighbor. Methodist societies reached out in love to the forgotten people of the world and ministered to them. At times, we United Methodists have been criticized for going too far in the spirit of love. Our stress upon the inclusiveness of the church has been a cause of conflict from time to time. We have been less interested in how many we can keep out than in how many we can draw in. Our vision of the church is one of inclusiveness rather than exclusiveness. Did not Jesus say, "And when I am lifted up from the earth, [I] will draw all [people] to myself" (John 12:32)?

Of course, sometimes we err, and our standards get reduced or blurred. We have problems with the tension between acceptance and accountability, inclusiveness and high standards. But love sometimes puts the welfare of the neighbor over high standards. Love is therefore messy, not too easily defined, but Jesus put it at the core of the church.

One can hear the Wesleyan emphasis on love in this great hymn of Charles Wesley, "Love Divine, All Loves Excelling"

> Love divine, all loves excelling,
> joy of heaven, to earth come down;
> fix in us thy humble dwelling;
> all thy faithful mercies crown!
> Jesus, thou art all compassion,
> pure, unbounded love thou art;
> visit us with thy salvation;
> enter every trembling heart.

Breathe, O breathe thy loving Spirit
into every troubled breast!
Let us all in thee inherit;
let us find that second rest.
Take away our bent to sinning;
Alpha and Omega be;
end of faith as its beginning,
Set our hearts at liberty.

Finish, then, thy new creation;
pure and spotless let us be.
Let us see thy great salvation
perfectly restored in thee;
changed from glory into glory,
till in heaven we take our place,
till we cast our crowns before thee,
lost in wonder, love, and praise.

A third United Methodist emphasis is *experience.*
Experience is the validation of our doctrine. At the same
time, we can't accept any and all experiences, no matter
how sincerely felt, as valid expressions of Christianity.
As we said earlier, we validate our individual experiences
by placing them against the backdrop of Scripture,
tradition, and reason. Our individual experiences must
submit to the wisdom and guidance of the larger church.
In our stress on experience, our goal is not merely to
receive the gospel as information, but to lead to personal
transformation and lifelong formation, "experimental"
religion as Wesley called it, "living faith."

Part of our ecumenical spirit can be attributed to our
emphasis upon experience. We have learned, in our own
lives, that the church lives and breathes as the sum of
many different experiences of God. Experience can also
be motivation for our evangelistic outreach. Because we
have experienced the love of God in our hearts, we try to

reach out and share it with others, overflowing with a desire to show and tell what God has done among us.

Religious experience for Wesley was never divorced from reason and restraint. Rather, experience is informed and enriched by theological insights about the traditions of the faith and by scientific insights about life, nature, and society. This was one reason that Wesley encouraged his people to write down accounts of their conversions and subsequent experiences of the grace of God, some of which he reproduced in his *Journal*. These could then be studied by the larger Christian community, analyzed, and properly interpreted. Albert Einstein once said, "Experience is not what happens to you, but what you do with what happens to you." True. But that is a bit too human-centered and subjective to capture what Wesley meant by "experience." Wesley might have said, "Experience is not just what happens to you, but what *God* does with what happens to you."

Church historian Leonard Sweet has said: "Wesley was not concerned whether your experience of God had the intensity of a flashlight or a floodlight. For each person it will be of different candlepower. He was only concerned that it was genuinely *your* experience of God, that it had authentic theological content, and that it led you to a community . . . God still makes cold hearts warm today, and provides for their continual warming."

One night, at a church meeting, I was asked by a somewhat billigerent person, "When and where were you converted to Christ?" It was, for him, a sort of litmus test for evangelical orthodoxy that I be able to cite the time and the place of my conversion to God in Christ. I took the question as a very United Methodist sort of theological question, a question which invited me to do some God-talk about my God-walk. I began as I have started in this book, with my infancy at McBee Chapel. Then I told of my adolescence among the good folk at

Buncombe Street Church. There was that magic night beside the lake at the South Carolina United Methodist (SCUM, the kids call it) Camp in the mountains. Then I recalled my days of growth in an invigorating undergraduate religion class at a United Methodist school, Wofford College. But could I forget the summer that I worked with youth at a United Methodist church and ended up learning more about God than I was able to teach? And then there was my first congregation, who showed me more about Christ's church than I had been able to learn in three years of seminary.

See? My conversion was a long, grace-filled process, the result of a lifelong walk with God, the sum of the gifts of many different people, something which was still in progress, moving to perfection.

> Finish, then, thy new creation;
> pure and spotless let us be.
> Let us see thy great salvation
> perfectly restored in thee.

In short, my (yet to be completed, thank God) conversion was a very United Methodist sort of theological experience. Growth in grace, it could be called.

CHAPTER SEVEN

BECAUSE RELIGION IS NOT A PRIVATE AFFAIR

I dare say most people join a church because they are attracted to some aspect of an individual congregation. They like the pastor, or they find a place in a Sunday school class, or their friends in the congregation ask them to join. And this is as it should be because the church occurs in specific, individual congregations.

But when you join a United Methodist congregation, in a sense you join every other United Methodist Congregation in the whole wide world because we are a people held together by *connectionalism.*

In true *congregationalism,* the individual congregation is a self-functioning, autonomous unit. The congregation stands or falls on what occurs within that congregation. In a *connectional church,* each congregation is connected to every other congregation. Our churches don't "call" or hire clergy; clergy are "appointed" to congregations by the Bishop in that area. When you give to the church, your gifts go far because they join with the gifts of nearly nine million others in a cooperative effort to minister to the needs of the whole world.

That which Wesley resolutely forbade in England, he allowed in America—the organization of an entirely new denomination. The specific occasion was Wesley's decision to ordain clergy for America in order to provide leadership for his "poor sheep in the wilderness." This position was arrived at only after much study and agony on Wesley's part. By 1784, American Methodists were a new church.

The founding Christmas Conference in 1784 made a number of decisions which determined the future of American Methodism. They decided (much to Wesley's dismay) that American Methodism would be an episcopal church, a church led by bishops. It would be a church which would have an itinerating ministry whose members would hold their membership within an Annual Conference rather than in individual congregations. Local congregations would be parts of circuits and of the larger connection. The structure would be sufficiently flexible to make the local congregation adaptable for mission in various situations.

Although it is natural that you would give your loyalty to your local congregation, every United Methodist is expected to support the work of the entire denomination. This means contributing funds to the work of the various agencies of the general church. This also means that the general church has a responsibility to each congregation.

To be United Methodist is to signal a willingness to be part of the life and direction of the whole denomination as determined by our leaders and official bodies. John Wesley set the tone for a church with a relatively high amount of centralized control. In the class meeting, individual members were subject to the scrutiny and discipline of the leaders. The leaders were held accountable to other leaders.

Today's clergy are accountable not just to the members of the congregation where they serve, but to the larger church and all their fellow clergy in the Annual Conference. This expanded accountability is our United Methodist way of encouraging high standards of clergy performance while at the same time ensuring the freedom of clergy to preach and to teach in ways which are faithful to the larger church, not just pleasing to the members of that congregation. More than once I have been personally grateful that my future as a United Methodist preacher was in the hands of my Bishop rather than with a majority vote of the congregation.

Our churches are accountable, not just to their own local standards of righteousness, but to the scrutiny of the larger church. For instance, when I was a child nearly all predominantly white Methodist churches in the Deep South were segregated. Although these congregations probably knew that someday, perhaps tomorrow, they ought to do something about the traditional, but blatantly unchristian, practice of racial segregation in God's house, little was done. Finally, in the 1950s the General Conference directed that no Methodist church would ever refuse entry to anyone on the basis of race. If you are going to be part of our family, the rest of the church said, you must swing open your doors to all. And that was that. Although there was controversy, some grumbling, it was clear that the church had spoken. Sometimes it takes a good shove from our brothers and sisters for us to do what is right. Our connectional approach to Christianity has been one of the most effective aspects of United Methodists in mission.

An interesting aspect of The United Methodist Church's connectionalism is that all deeds to individual congregations are property of the Annual Conference. Sometimes our people have gotten angry about this peculiarity, but more than once it has saved our church. If a dissident group tries to take over a United Methodist congregation, or if a congregation fails to practice United Methodist doctrine or tries to leave the denomination, the Conference, through the Bishop, can step in and take the property. As a consequence, we have had a minimum of church breakups.

By working together, we do far more good than we could do alone. For instance, fifty years ago we created the United Methodist Committee on Overseas Relief (UMCOR). The purpose of UMCOR is "to alleviate suffering out of Christian conviction," specializing in immediate relief, rehabilitation for suffering persons, elimination of the root causes of hunger, and a wide array of refugee ministry. Through UMCOR, we are at work in more than 80 countries. Because of our worldwide network of missionaries and local congregations within the world Methodist family, about ninety-nine cents of every dollar given to UMCOR goes directly into relief. So we are at work rebuilding flood ravaged Bangladesh, resettling Haitian refugees in the U.S.A., developing war-torn Mozambique, offering assistance to hurricane and earthquake victims in the states, and feeding children in Nepal. Although you may never have left Des Moines, through the worldwide network of United Methodists in mission, you serve around the globe.

ORGANIZED RELIGION

Many Americans are suspicious of institutions and organizations. The lives of many feel constrained and regulated by a host of impersonal, cold, bureaucratic agencies. As we have said, we Americans tend to be rugged individualists who jealously guard our personal prerogatives and prefer to function with a minimum of organizational, governmental, and bureaucratic interventions.

Is it any wonder then that many Americans are suspicious of big, highly organized, structurally complex churches? Have we not said, in the very first chapter of this book, that religion is of the heart, a matter of deeply felt emotion and personally experienced faith? Did not Jesus criticize those who followed the various external forms of religion while allowing the spirit of religion to grow cold within their own lives? Were not some of

Jesus' most severe critics the stilted bureaucrats from the religious establishment? Is it any wonder then that many modern people say they have had it with "organized religion"? Americans seem to be just as "religious" as ever if by "religious" we mean that they still say that they believe in God, pray, and expect an afterlife. But our mainline churches are declining in numbers. Americans are "believers but not joiners" says Lutheran historian Martin Marty. We're into religion as a private, personal affair but not as an institutional, organizational affair.

If this is the case, then we United Methodists, for all our warmheartedness, have a big problem. For if ever there were an organized, institutionalized church, it is ours.

We have a rule, or at least a committee, for just about everything. Every cause has its caucus. We do our business strictly "by the book" (*The Book of Discipline,* that is). Thumb through our *Discipline* and you will find rules for the making (and unmaking) of clergy, buying and selling of property, taking a vote, and taking a stand. Every year, each pastor and congregation must make a detailed report of what was done in that church in the past year and present it to the District Superintendent and Bishop. Every pastor's salary must be reported to the whole Annual Conference. Every congregation is expected to bear a proportional burden of the cost of running the whole worldwide United Methodist Church. We are, or at least try to be, *organized* religion.

Our penchant for rules, procedures, committees, and structure gives rise to jokes of the "How-many-United-Methodists-does-it-take-to-change-a-light-bulb?" variety. So, in a society which is dubious about the value of form, structure, and organization, it behooves us United Methodists to explain ourselves a bit. Why all this organization? Why can't we just get together, praise the Lord, and do our best to serve God?

Well, first of all, our spiritual father was John Wesley, who wasn't called a "Methodist" for nothing. Wesley did not give up his disciplined, highly organized ways after his Aldersgate experience. In fact, his "heart-warming" experience intensified his efforts to find a suitable structure, a practical method, to enable ordinary people to experience the full graciousness of God.

To the warm heart Wesley added a system of daily, small-group-supported, spiritual disciplines. In fact, organization was perhaps Wesley's greatest talent. As some have said, Wesley's friend George Whitefield was a much more popular and inspiring preacher than Wesley. When Whitefield died, he left behind converts and believers. Wesley's legacy was a church.

Jesus' message was not a simple "Do you agree?" or "Do you feel?" but "Will you join up?" Will you come forward to become part of a movement, a people? So being a Christian is more than a vague feeling or intellectual assent. It is also discipleship, discipline, embodiment. The church is the very Body of Christ, the specific, institutional, corporate, in the flesh form which the Risen Christ has chosen to take in the world. This doesn't deny that Christ may take a variety of forms to be present in the world. It affirms that Christ's promised, predominant presence is in and through the organizational church. The United Methodist Church is one of its (most organized) aspects.

Wesley had no interest, nor should we, in organization for its own sake. We are (one nineteenth-century observer said of us) "organized to beat the devil." Our organization is for the sake of mission. This whole complex, beautiful structure rises or falls on how well or poorly it helps us get the job done. The ever practical Wesley created a whole range of new structures to get the job done in eighteenth-century England, many of which still help United Methodists get the job done today.

Frustrated by the lethargy and unavailability of the trained, professional clergy to reach the impoverished masses, Wesley reluctantly consented to appoint unordained lay persons to preach, to organize Methodist societies, and to teach. If the established seminaries would not educate these well-intentioned but untrained *lay preachers*, Wesley would educate them himself by devising a rigorous program of reading for them. A lone figure on horseback, reading a copy of Wesley's *Sermons*, became a familiar sight in Wesley's England and in the new lands of North America. Today, United Methodists still utilize "local pastors," persons who come into the pastoral ministry, often later in life, and are trained by the church for service as part-time or full-time pastors. United Methodist deployment of lay leadership at all levels of church life continues our heritage of a church for the people and led by the people.

One of the most impressive Wesleyan organizational inventions was his *Societies*. These small groups met weekly for prayer, Bible reading, and communal discipline. Members were urged to continue to be faithful in their attendance at their local Anglican church—Methodism was not a church but a movement of reform within that church. Failure to live up to the high moral precepts of the Society resulted in expulsion. Eventually, Wesley organized these far-flung groups into The United Societies which the sometimes authoritarian and dogmatic Mr. Wesley totally controlled, including the appointment and assignment of his traveling lay preachers.

Societies were composed of *Class Meetings*, a group of twelve persons under the care of a lay leader. These were small, intimate, caring, but highly disciplined groups whose members aided one another to "grow in grace" and thus provided the institutional and organizational embodiment for Wesley's concern for sanctification and lifelong Christian growth.

While the Societies with their Class Meetings eventually evolved into a full-fledged denomination, the Wesleyan small group tradition lives on in the Sunday school classes, innumerable bible study, prayer, and work groups which any United Methodist Church comprises. Church Growth strategists note that, to grow, a congregation must constantly create new small groups. There is no such thing as a large church, only large numbers of small groups who happen to gather in the same building. As Mr. Wesley discovered, the church, no matter how big it becomes, is still primarily a face-to-face meeting of friends who know and care about one another.

Alcoholics Anonymous, or A.A., has proved to be one of the most effective means in the world of combatting the terrible ravages of alcoholism. The individual alcoholic joins with others who acknowledge that addiction to alcohol is ruining their lives. They realize that they can't pull this off alone. They know that they need one another and God to lick the problem.

At the beginning of an A.A. meeting, persons introduce themselves by saying, "I am Joe. I am an alcoholic"; "I am Jane. I am an alcoholic." No one lectures them; they refuse to lecture one another. They simply tell their stories with honesty and anonymity. They tell where they went wrong and how they are trying to go right. They tell where they find the power and the hope to keep trying. Sometimes one of them will take special responsibility for another, promising to be ready, day or night, if need arises. That's about all there is to A.A.; yet thereby, in the small A.A. group, miracles occur. Wesley discovered the miracle of the small, convenanted, honest, caring group long before A.A. Where two or three are gathered, there is Jesus, there is power, there is life.

But early Methodist organization meant much more than settling in to cozy, like-minded small groups. To keep the Methodists on the move, Wesley assigned his preachers to geographic *circuits*. A preacher traveled about from place to place in his circuit, organizing, preaching, counseling, teaching. This method of clergy deployment proved to be sheer genius when applied to the American frontier. From the coastal cities, Methodist circuit riders spread out, moving ever westward, into the frontier. Preachers were never allowed to settle in and become comfortable and cozy in one location. Bishops kept them on the move, just as Wesley had kept his riders moving. This, more than anything else, accounts for why United Methodists are found today in every corner of our continent. No sooner was a congregation established somewhere than the circuit was reorganized and the traveling preacher sent somewhere that had no church.

Circuit riders had tough lives by our standards. At first, marriage was prohibited, later, only begrudgingly accepted. Most circuit riders met an early death. "I wish my circuit riders were as strong as their horses," complained one early Bishop.

The circuit rider tradition continues today. A large number of our clergy serve a number of congregations at the same time, jumping in their Toyota and riding from one Sunday service to the next. All of our clergy are still appointed to a pastoral charge only one year at a time, although most remain at that church (or churches) for as many as four years or more. Persons who come to our denomination from a church which has a "call" system of clergy deployment (the individual congregation selects and hires its pastor) may wonder why we move our ministers in this way in our episcopal system (the bishop and cabinet appoint the pastor to the congregation). Like every form of church organization, ours has its pluses and minuses.

Advantages of the United Methodist Clergy
Appointment System

1. Every church, no matter how small or cantankerous, is assured of a pastor. The congregation itself doesn't have to waste energy and resources hunting or haggling to get a pastor.

2. Pastors are assigned on the basis of the bishop's (assisted by the district superintendent's) assessment of that congregation's missional needs rather than on the basis of how much the congregation can pay or on the basis of a few powerful people's wishes. Sometimes this means that the pastor you get is the one you *need* rather than simply the one you like.

3. If it's a bad marriage of pastor and congregation (sometimes the bishop's idea of a perfect match is mistaken) both pastor and congregation can be delivered of each other by the bishop without all the messiness of firing.

4. Finally, to be utterly honest, even if your present pastor is not the worst preacher in the world, but far from the best, be patient. Conference meets every year so there's a good chance that you will soon be delivered.

Disadvantages

1. There are some congregations that ought to be forced to face the fact that no preacher in his or her right mind would eagerly come to them. They ought to get their act together rather than always expect the bishop to look after them.

2. Despite the bishop's best intention, even bishops goof up and send the wrong pastor to the wrong church.

3. Because our clergy appointment system is essentially a clergy-run system, sometimes the bishop and the clergy appear to be more concerned about looking after fellow clergy than undergirding the mission of the

congregation. We United Methodists are perhaps "going on to perfection," but we are not there yet. This is not, despite our best efforts, a perfect world.

So, according to my count, the score is four in favor, three against. By a majority of one, it's all in all a system which United Methodists, though we sometimes complain, still live with and continue to feel is a valid means of ministry.

A final Wesleyan organizational innovation was his creation of a yearly Conference. Wesley gathered his traveling preachers each year for intense worship, study, and discussion, all under the strong hand of Wesley himself. This tradition is continued in the *Annual Conference* where now both laity and clergy from every church in that Conference gather to worship, talk (lots of talk), make reports (lots of them), vote, plan, and get renewed for another year of work. Although Wesley would probably not approve, now United Methodist lay delegates to Conference vote on everything except those matters which relate only to the clergy themselves.

We also have five *Jurisdictional Conferences* (composed of several Annual Conferences by geographic areas) where our bishops are elected. Outside the United States, our denomination is organized according to *Central Conferences.* Every four years, *General Conference* gathers—the basic, national, legislative body of our church. Through its debates, resolutions, legislation, and votes, General Conference is the only body that speaks for our church in an official, public, legal way.

In the day-to-day life of a congregation, the average United Methodist is little aware of all this organization and structure which lies behind his or her church. However, aware of it or not, this connected, cooperative, worldwide structure is probably the most distinguishing mark of United Methodism. Our legislation ensures order and fairness in our life together. Because of our rules for everything, individual congregations need not "reinvent the wheel" every time they purchase property, or desire to participate in foreign mission, or need to resolve some difficult internal dispute. Time need not be wasted while the individual congregation flounders about in the mire of petty procedural matters. Our *Discipline* gives us fair, tested, grace-filled guidance. Linked together in the connection, stronger congregations help weaker ones; people in one geographical area are bound in love and service to other United Methodists across the country. We do far more good together than we could do on our own. Our organization keeps us in mission, prods us to look beyond our own merely local horizons, and challenges us to keep up with the continuing movements of a living God.

Once, when one of our congregation's visiting evangelistic teams was calling upon a prospective member, the prospective member said, "I'm not interested in organized religion. I believe my religion is my own business."

"Well, then you ought to love Trinity Church," said the unshaken visitation team member. "We've been trying to get ourselves organized for thirty years and it hasn't happened yet."

Whether or not we really get it together as United Methodists, we certainly try, seeing our organizational life together as the means of mission, the form which the Risen Christ has chosen to take among us.

WE'RE ALL IN THIS TOGETHER

The great heresy of American popular religion is the notion that religion is a private affair, a purely personal matter of individual opinion. Many critics of our culture have noted the subjective, individualized nature of our society. We are fragmented into lone individuals, a nation of strangers, each person zealously guarding his or her rights and personal prerogatives while feeling little or no responsibility for other persons. We have our freedom, but also much loneliness.

So individuals shop around for a religious enclave that "meets my needs," turning religion into yet another item for personal consumption. Sunday morning church is described as a "filling station," a place where I come to get my needs fulfilled, my spirit serviced for another week. We judge all experiences, people, ideas on the basis of personal fulfillment—What's in it for *me*?

The Christian church, in this cultural context, can degenerate into a center for therapy, a place to discuss assorted religious ideas, or a stage for religious entertainment. If this cafeteria-line approach to religion is criticized, the response is, "Well, at least they are meeting people's needs."

We United Methodists are committed to meeting human need. John Wesley set the tone for us in his creative adaptation of the church for Christian mission. But Christian mission involves meeting human needs *in the name of Christ*. That makes all the difference because the gospel rearranges our definitions of "human need."

In a superficial, pathless culture, many people may feel that their greatest need is for some spiritual "high," some means of momentarily alleviating the boredom brought on by a life without purpose. Or others may think that their greatest need is for a sort of spiritual narcotic, something to soothe the pain, if only for a time. The gospel judges our desires (which we often define as "need") and teaches us what is worth wanting in life, what is worth living for, what is worth dying for.

The connectional approach of United Methodism collides with the values of our do-your-own-thing, radically subjectivized, self-centered culture. It demands that we become grafted to a family, a worldwide people whose membership transcends national boundaries and divisions of race and class. Because we are a connected church, we are constantly prodded beyond the narrow confines of our own individual aches and pains, and invited to share the burden of some of the world's need. In a connected church, we meet people, strange people—strangers whom we might have avoided if left to our own devices—and we learn to call them "sister," "brother."

As we noted earlier, one of John Wesley's great insights was that the Christian life, if taken seriously, is far too demanding to live alone. Perhaps some saint might be able to walk the way of the cross in isolation, but saints are few and far between. Most of us need help from our friends. If all the Christian life involves is a momentary realization of God's saving grace (justification), then who needs friends for that? But if (as Wesley contended) the Christian life also involves maturation and growth in grace (sanctification), then you can never do it by yourself.

One of the great hymns of the Methodist societies is still sung at the opening of our Annual Conferences. It expresses, more poetically than can I, that we are all in this together, amazed as it says, that we are yet alive:

> And are we yet alive,
> and see each other's face?
> Glory and thanks to Jesus give
> For his almighty grace!
>
> Preserved by power divine
> to full salvation here,
> again in Jesus' praise we join,
> and in his sight appear.
>
> What troubles have we seen,
> what mighty conflicts past,
> fightings without, and fears within,
> Since we assembled last!

Yet out of all the Lord
hath brought us by his love;
and still he doth his help afford,
and hides our life above.

Then let us make our boast
of his redeeming power,
which saves us to the uttermost,
Till we can sin no more;

Let us take up the cross,
till we the crown obtain,
and gladly reckon all things loss,
so we may Jesus gain.

Although Methodism has greatly neglected, and can even be said to have lost Wesley's emphasis upon the small group, there is a possibility of recovery. The Church Growth Movement, for instance, stresses that individuals must be linked to some small group within a church in order to be truly integrated into the church. People respond to face-to-face, small group situations. If it is true that Christians in today's world face a great challenge in maintaining their faith and disciplining their lives, there is no better vehicle than the small group—Sunday school classes, prayer groups, and all the other groups through which Christians aid other Christians in their daily walk with Christ.

Religion is not, never can be, wasn't meant to be a private affair because (1) Jesus called, not isolated individuals, but a group of disciples, bound them together in love, and told them to stick together as his Body in this world (I Cor. 12–13); (2) Jesus blessed ordinary people so that they might go forth to be a blessing for others, to go out and heal, cast out demons, feed the hungry, and show forth the good news in word and deed (Luke 10:1-22).

Why am I a United Methodist? At the beginning I admitted that I am first of all a United Methodist today because a number of people put me here yesterday. I called it a gift, an act of grace. No doubt God might have saved me through any number of other devices. The Bible shows God to be infinitely resourceful and creative in getting his way. However, it appears that God has chosen to get his way with me through The United Methodist Church. Perhaps it will be the same for you.

In sum, I find that United Methodism has five great gifts to offer our troubled, but still blessed and beloved-by-God world:

(1) Stress on the need for a personal, engaging, experienced relationship with Christ. (We can *know* *Christ*, not just know about Christ.)

(2) The need for structure, discipline, and form in meeting the challenges of living a Christian life today. (Some things are too important to be left to chance.)

(3) The importance of lifelong journey and self-examination, assisted by others, in developing our lives in Christ. (We can actually grow and be better people than we are right now.)

(4) The refusal to separate spiritual needs from human, material needs. (God loves whole persons, not just detached "souls.")

(5) The stress upon the church, its proclamation, sacraments, and other "ordinary means of grace" against our rampant individualism and subjectivism. (Religion—the Christian one, that is—is *not* a private affair.)

We're not at all smug about these unique United Methodist contributions. After all, we received them as gifts, grace, in what happened to a proper little Oxford don at Aldersgate Street, or in what happened to improper little me at a sprawling, downtown cathedral of a church called Buncombe Street.

When I was a child, growing up in Buncombe Street Church, a missionary came to visit us. She met with all the children and told us that she was *our* missionary in China. She described to us how, when she was still a child in Iowa, at about our age, she gave her life to Christ to spread the Good News, in word and deed, around the world, wherever God would send her. Then she showed us a small, beautifully decorated black box full of cooked rice. She told us that this little box held the average daily amount of rice that was given to a Chinese child. What if we had to live on that amount of food a day?

She then suggested that, as a sign of our Christian commitment, we lay aside a penny a day, denying ourselves a candy bar for a week, to feed the children whom God loved in China.

"But aren't those *Communist* children in China?" someone of us asked.

"Well, perhaps that's what some of their parents might say," replied the missionary. "But you and I know that they're, first and last, *God's* children, maybe someday even Methodist children."

I couldn't have been more than seven or eight. But that missionary made a deep impression on me. She was *my* missionary, working for *me* in a place I would never see among people I would never meet, making them brothers and sisters. I began saving my pennies with the other children, and each month we mailed our gifts. I never thought about God's people in China the same way after that. I never thought about myself the same way either.

This, I believe, was a typically United Methodist experience which has resulted in a typically United Methodist person like me.

I remember attending a service at St. Paul's Cathedral in London, familiar haunt of John and Charles Wesley.

The bulletin explaining the service said something like, "In entering this cathedral, you have entered a conversation which began long before you were born and which shall continue long after you are dead."

That conversation across the generations is our church as well. I have been a part of it; so have you. As heirs of John Wesley, Philip William Otterbein, Jacob Albright, Susanna Wesley, Mary McLeod Bethune, and all the others who marched in this great procession, let us show the same resourcefulness, the same creativity and courage in methodically living out the gospel in our day as they showed in theirs. Let us not merely preserve our church, but examine it, change it, prod it, to keep putting mission above mere maintenance.

Toward the end of his life, Wesley urged his people to influence the world through the example of their own manner of life together because, when all's said and done, the best witness the church has to the truth of its claims is *the church*, your church, St. John's on the Expressway or wherever there is a group of people which visibly embodies the Gospel.

Wesley exhorted his people, as God's primary vehicle for affecting the world. He wrote to his followers: "In the meantime, let all those who are real members of the Church, see that they walk holy and unblamable in all things. 'Ye are the light of the world!' Ye are 'a city set upon a hill' and 'cannot be hid.' O 'let your light shine before men!' Show them your faith by your works. Let them see, by the whole tenor of your conversation, that your hope is all laid up above! Let all our words and actions evidence the spirit whereby you are animated! Above all things, let your love abound. Let it extend to every child of man: Let it overflow to every child of God. By this let all know whose disciples you are because you 'love one another' " (Jackson, *Works*, pp. 400-401).

LEARNING GUIDE

This book is one person's perspective on what it is like to be a United Methodist. I hope it gives individual United Methodists a new appreciation for who they are. I also hope that this book will be given to prospective United Methodists, earnest inquirers, visitors, critics, or anyone else who wants to know more about us. After all, we are big on education. That could happen alone or in a group—an inquirers group of potential new members, a prayer and study group, a Sunday school class, a confirmation class. The chapters are short enough to be read in one sitting and each can stand on its own.

Whether you use this book alone or in a small-group setting over a period of weeks, here are some suggested learning activities for each chapter:

ONE—RELIGION IS OF THE HEART

1. Can you point to an experience in your life, similar to what John Wesley felt at Aldersgate? Share this with your group.

2. Try to give some concrete, every day examples of your own experience of the following: *Prevenient Grace, Justifying Grace, Sanctifying Grace.*

3. With a copy of our *Hymnal* identify those hymns that speak of the three aspects of God's grace which Wesley emphasized.

TWO—THE BIBLE IS OUR BOOK

1. If asked, "Which Bible story or passage has meant the most to you?" how would you respond? Share with the group.

2. In what ways do you think the Bible provokes a "head-on collision with our preconceptions and limited, self-centered opinions"?

3. Can you think of examples where the church is putting the words of the Bible into faithful action today?

THREE—RELIGION IS PRACTICAL

1. What do you believe to be the chief personal, social, or family issue with which people need practical help from the church? How could the church help?

2. Design a banner which contains symbols or images for the ways in which your church "Makes Disciples."

FOUR—CHRISTIANS ARE TO WORSHIP

1. If worship is "the very center of the church," what do you feel is at the very center, the most important aspect, the whole point of worship?

2. Discuss some of the ways in which the worship and preaching of our church are an experience of Wesley's "ordinary means of grace."

3. Go through a copy of your church's order of worship and identify the most meaningful and the least meaningful aspects of your church's worship. Why do you respond to these parts as you do?

FIVE—CHRISTIANS ARE TO WITNESS

1. Do a role playing situation in which one of you is a friend who is considering a visit to your church and have another member of your group tell his/her friend some good reasons to visit.

2. On the way out of church one Sunday, a fellow church member says to you, "I wish that our pastor would stop meddling in controversial issues that are none of the church's business." Take turns discussing how you might respond as a United Methodist.

SIX—CHRISTIANS ARE TO GROW

1. Discuss ways in which you have experienced United Methodism drawing upon other denominations and groups that have influenced it—The Church of England, the Moravians, the Evangelical United Brethren, the Puritans, the Evangelicals, Roman Catholics.

2. In your group, discuss some contemporary ethical problem (abortion, nuclear arms, etc.). Apply each aspect of the Wesleyan quadrilateral to the problem. Now, check to see if this problem is discussed in our *Discipline*.

SEVEN—RELIGION IS NOT A PRIVATE AFFAIR

1. As a group, list the advantages and disadvantages of United Methodism as a connectional church. What is the score?

2. What are some of the ways in which the church could do a better job of providing its members with

structural, group support for the challenges of being a Christian today?

3. Talk about what you like and dislike about being a United Methodist. What are the easiest aspects? the most difficult? If you have ever been a member of another denomination, share why you became interested in The United Methodist Church.

INDEX

CPSIA information can be obtained at www.ICGtesting.com
Printed in the USA
LVOW11s1421290715

448004LV00020B/106/P

9 780687 453566